FAITH AND ORDER IN THE U.S.A.

Faith and Order in the U.S.A.

A Brief History of
Studies and Relationships

William A. Norgren

William B. Eerdmans Publishing Company

Grand Rapids, Michigan / Cambridge, U.K.

Published 2011 by
Wm. B. Eerdmans Publishing Co.
2140 Oak Industrial Drive N.E., Grand Rapids, Michigan 49505 /
P.O. Box 163, Cambridge CB3 9PU U.K.

Printed in the United States of America

17 16 15 14 13 12 11   7 6 5 4 3 2 1

Library of Congress Cataloging-in-Publication Data

Norgren, William A.
Faith and Order in the U.S.A.: a brief history of studies and relationships /
William A. Norgren.
p.   cm.
ISBN 978-0-8028-6599-1 (pbk.: alk. paper)
1. National Council of the Churches of Christ in the United States of America.
Commission on Faith and Order — History — 20th century.
2. Christian union — United States — History — 20th century.
3. United States — Church history — 20th century.   I. Title.

BX6.N2N67   2011

280'.042 — dc22

2011005875

www.eerdmans.com

Contents

Author's Note

No single imagination can truly own the story of Faith and Order in twentieth-century America. It is rather a matter of clearing a space in one's mind where certain happenings may be identified and reconvened.

For the period between the North American Conference on Faith and Order in 1957 until 1971, Part I of this account draws on the archives and on service as first director of Faith and Order Studies of the National Council of the Churches of Christ in the U.S.A. As the archives of the council are inaccessible after 1971, Part II relies on ecumenical journals, recent files at the Faith and Order office, and on service in the ecumenical office of the Episcopal Church from 1974 to 1999.

Thanks are due the Presbyterian Historical Society, depository for National Council of Churches archives, and Faith and Order directors Jeffrey Gros, Norman A. Hjelm, William G. Rusch, Ann K. Riggs, and Antonios Kireopoulos for their guidance. The content of this history is solely the author's responsibility.

Over the years it has been an extraordinary privilege and blessing to know and to learn from Christians nurtured in so many traditions and cultures. I hope and believe that such experiences of catholicity will become ever more widespread among members of Christ's body.

CHAPTER I

From the Beginning

Churches in America took part in the Faith and Order movement from the beginning. Missionary Bishop Charles Henry Brent, present at the landmark World Missionary Conference at Edinburgh in 1910, saw that faithfulness to the church's mission required the separated churches not only to cooperate but also to face issues of faith and church order dividing them. That same year Brent inspired the General Convention of the Episcopal Church to resolve "that a joint commission be appointed to bring about a conference for the consideration of questions touching Faith and Order, and that all Christian Communions throughout the world which confess our Lord Jesus Christ as God and Savior be asked to unite with us in arranging for and conducting such a conference." The work of corresponding with other churches fell to influential layman Robert H. Gardiner, secretary of the commission and later first secretary of Faith and Order. Another influential layman, financier J. Pierpont Morgan, contributed $100,000 to support the movement.

At the same time Peter Ainslie of the Christian Church (Disciples of Christ), itself founded as a movement to foster Christian unity, called for "a World Conference on matters of Christian unity among all churches." Many churches responded by appointing cooperating commissions. Negotiations with leaders in Europe and the Middle East led to an international continuation committee. But the catastrophe of the First World War intervened. The World Conference on Faith and Order did not meet until 1927 at Lausanne, chaired by Brent. World conferences followed in 1937 at Edinburgh and in 1952 at Lund, Sweden. Faith and Order became part of the World Council of Churches at its foundation in 1948.

At Lund a new policy was initiated that would have special significance for North America. At any world meeting the issues are inevitably generalized to some degree. So it is difficult to do justice to the very different balance of church traditions found on major continents or to the many complex cultural, social, and political factors that condition the life and thought of churches in each time and place. Lund encouraged regional councils of churches to project programs of study, taking into account the divisive and unitive forces that operate in each region, yet without neglecting the world perspective.

The Nature of the Unity We Seek

The initiative was taken by the U.S. Conference of the World Council of Churches, which invited the Canadian Council of Churches and the National Council of the Churches of Christ in the U.S.A. to join in sponsoring a North American Conference on Faith and Order. Protestant, Anglican, and Orthodox churches were members of the councils, but conservative Evangelical, Pentecostal, Adventist, and Holiness churches were not. A broad participation was sought through local preparatory studies. Sixteen cities of different sizes and types were chosen for study groups composed of persons with competence to deal with the assigned topics, and these lasted a year and a half. In addition, a special group of theologians and sociologists was selected to study population mobility and the consequent shifting of denominational affiliations. A further 350 groups were organized by state and local councils, ministerial associations, Church Women United, and in colleges and seminaries. All this experience led to a demand at the national conference for more continuous and systematic programs of Faith and Order in national, state, and local councils of churches.

When the North American conference met at Oberlin, Ohio, in 1957 for a week of intensive study, thirty-eight Canadian and U.S.

churches were represented. Observers from other churches were present together with consultants and staff. Bishop Angus Dun was elected chairman, Eugene Carson Blake and Emlyn Davies were elected vice-chairmen, and J. Robert Nelson recording secretary. Representatives of four North American theological commissions created by World Council Faith and Order after the Lund conference spoke at Oberlin on Christ and the Church, Tradition and Traditions, Institutionalism, and Worship. The twelve conference sections worked from papers produced by the city study groups. They prepared reports on their topics and shaped reports from the three divisions in which they were grouped. All the addresses and reports were edited by conference director Paul Minear and published in *The Nature of the Unity We Seek*.[1]

The Oberlin report reflects the current study of the doctrine of the church and is a remarkable analysis of the mid-century situation of the churches represented and of their hopes for visible unity. Titles of the three division reports convey an idea of its scope: In Faithfulness to the Eternal Gospel, In Terms of Organizational Structures, and In View of Cultural Pressures. Oberlin was the most inclusive gathering of North American churches to date, yet its Message to the churches expressed regret over "the absence of members of other churches whom we recognize as fellow Christians." Just two years later Pope John XXIII would announce an ecumenical council that would bring the Roman Catholic Church into the ecumenical movement, but the insights and gifts of conservative Evangelical, Pentecostal, Adventist, and Holiness churches would remain largely apart.

Oberlin did not attempt an ecclesiology; rather it asked what is the nature of the unity to be sought. Orthodox Church representatives affirmed the importance of such studies but explained that unity is for them a given unity that has never been lost and is embodied in the Orthodox Church, which has maintained the integrity of the apostolic faith and apostolic order. The whole conference was able to declare, "Our basic unity is in Jesus Christ, and we believe the Church, as the

---

1. Paul Minear, ed., *The Nature of the Unity We Seek* (St. Louis: Bethany Press, 1958).

fellowship (koinonia) of Christ's followers throughout all time and in every place, has been called into being by God . . . it is more than a social institution. It is an ordered community whose Head is Christ, and it is the Body of Christ." The apostolic task of the churches is "to witness to the Gospel and to bring its redeeming power to bear upon every aspect of human life. For this task it has been given an ordered life of Word, sacraments and ministry which is to be exercised in and by the power of the Holy Spirit."[2]

Oberlin characterized the situation with regard to church order and organization in this way:

> The Church by its very nature exists in history with a visible structure, derived from the divine revelation given in Christ. . . . [The] visible reality of the Church involves its given function as well as its organizational embodiment. At the dimension of given function we have a large measure of agreement. At the dimension of organizational embodiment we may have varying structures but do not regard these as insuperable barriers to union. . . . Stubborn differences, however, separate us in our understanding of another matter involving both those dimensions. These have to do with the Church's order, and particularly the sacraments and the ministry . . . further understanding and common study (are called for) if we are to move toward unity in visible structure.[3]

Nevertheless, "[w]here churches possess a similar understanding of the nature of the Church and the ministry, steps toward organizational unity may be called for as a fuller expression of the deeper unity which is our common goal." In every case a plan of organic union "must be based on a clear understanding of the faith of the whole church."[4]

The Message to the churches briefly summarizes the Oberlin findings about the nature of the unity we seek. It is "in Christ," "in adora-

2. Minear, *Nature*, p. 206.
3. Minear, *Nature*, p. 207.
4. Minear, *Nature*, p. 210.

tion of God," "of declared faith," "of bearing one another's burdens and sharing one another's joys," "in which every ministry is a ministry of and for all the members, bound together in a worshiping and sacramental community," "in mission to the world," and "possessing a rich variety in worship, life and organization."[5]

Considered as a whole, the Oberlin report suggests three conclusions. First, Oberlin moves beyond the idea of an organizational federation of Protestant denominations by affirming an "essential order" of the church, about which "stubborn differences" persist. In this connection the role of councils of churches comes under analysis, both as witnesses to the unity of the church beyond the boundaries of denominations and as limited social fellowships that may not be mistaken for Christian unity.

Second, Oberlin understood that it is not enough that Christian unity find expression only in supra-local terms and forms but must do so in the places where people live. Training of congregations in ecumenical consciousness and responsibility "must be increasingly realized before any plan or plans of union can hope to be truly effective."[6] In this connection the conference affirmed: "It is not only our separations as churches and denominations but in our social stratification, our racial segregation, our introversion and self-content despite God's summons to our mission in the world, that we deny and refuse the uniting he would offer us."[7] In other words, increased ecumenical consciousness and responsibility and the growth of interdependence among congregations would lead to wider horizons of catholicity.

Third, the task of seeking unity can seem overwhelming because of its complexity. Oberlin says that "real Christian unity is more a process than a condition. It is primarily a sense of relatedness, a knowledge of belonging; and more, it is the exercise of that sense and that knowledge. If unity is only status or condition, if its manifestation is taken for the thing itself, then we might be tempted to allow the cultural pressures we feel to call it forth. We might think *we* can build it,

5. Minear, *Nature*, p. 29.
6. Minear, *Nature*, p. 238.
7. Minear, *Nature*, p. 29.

5

and we might try to build it out of necessity or expediency."[8] In other words, the unity we seek is the gift of God. God works through human life and actions, but "human structures and manipulations are not decisive."[9] This understanding suggests a larger place for ecumenical spirituality, prayer for unity, and shared worship.

The American Scene

The Oberlin conference recommended that a more permanent structure be established "to serve the churches in the U.S.A. in their common concerns for aspects of Faith and Order peculiar to the American scene, and as may enhance their participation, separately and together, in the concerns of Faith and Order of the whole ecumenical movement."[10] Before we turn to the post-Oberlin period we need to look back at unitive movements and certain cultural developments over the previous century and a half.[11]

Save for Native Americans, this is a nation of immigrants who brought their churches with them, rooted in different doctrinal, ethnic, and national traditions. Religious freedom and revivalism in the new nation also encouraged the creation of new churches, particularly on the frontier. This plurality of Christian bodies in America is unequaled anywhere in the world except perhaps in Brazil. Some bodies are large and some quite small, but all possess independent structures and authorities. *The Yearbook of American Churches* lists more than 250 bodies, although the majority of Christians are to be found in the twelve or so largest. No one church retained the loyalty of a large majority of the population in any region of the nation. It is a common-

8. Minear, *Nature*, p. 242.
9. Minear, *Nature*, p. 243.
10. Minear, *Nature*, p. 212.
11. These historical observations draw in part on *The Ecclesiological Significance of Councils of Churches: A Working Paper Prepared by the National Study Commission on the Ecclesiological Significance of Councils of Churches* (New York: National Council of Churches, 1963).

place that churches took on some of the aspects of sects, and sects of churches, or more accurately both became denominations.

Dissatisfied with the status quo, some Christians in the early nineteenth century thought that Protestants had much in common and that certain undertakings in cooperation were possible. They founded nondenominational agencies such as the American Bible Society, the American Sunday School Union, and the United Foreign Missionary Society to draw Christians together for fellowship and common tasks. Similar arrangements were made to influence American society, for example the Anti-Slavery Society, the American Education Society, tract societies, and temperance societies. Their influence had to be indirect, primarily through shaping public opinion. Following the same pattern, the YMCA and YWCA flourished as nondenominational lay efforts. These vast voluntary societies demonstrated that a single denomination could not do all the work of the church. The intense individualism and stress on freedom characteristic of nineteenth-century life, and the popularity of the evangelical-pietist concept of the church as a voluntary society, meant that the nondenominational agency way of providing the additional work satisfied most Protestants.

Many non-Protestants arrived in the later nineteenth century. The expanding cities with their patterns of pluralism and secularism made it more difficult for Protestants to influence public opinion. In the new situation the churches reached out to each other to form *inter*denominational agencies of cooperation such as the Foreign Missions Conference of North America, the Missionary Education Movement, the Home Missions Council, and the Sunday School Council of Evangelical Denominations. Early in the twentieth century Protestant churches formed the Federal Council of Churches and hundreds of state and local councils of churches. These fulfilled purposes similar to those of the nondenominational societies, but the sovereignty of the denominations, understood in juridical rather than theological terms, was carefully safeguarded. Most found they could cooperate in councils without significant changes in their theological positions, but Presbyterians had some difficulties while Lutherans and Episcopalians had more.

In 1950 the National Council of the Churches of Christ in the U.S.A. was founded by twenty-eight Protestant, Orthodox, and Episcopal churches through the merger of the old Federal Council and seven other interdenominational agencies. The National Council was once described as the most complex and intricate ecclesiastical machinery this planet has ever witnessed, but the inclusion of a wider range of churches brought interdenominational cooperation to a new level. It should be noted that while all member churches participated in the central general assembly and general board, they could and did participate in and fund only those they considered appropriate among the program units for global mission, international affairs, home mission, relief and development, racial inclusion, Christian education and Bible translation, stewardship, and evangelism.

Cooperation was the dominant unitive movement in America, but there were also calls for church union. The Christian Church (Disciples of Christ) was formed in 1832 and pledged to bring about the unity of all Christians. As early as 1838 Samuel Simon Schmucker appealed for federal union involving cooperation and intercommunion without affecting the authority, polity, or discipline of the churches. He renewed the appeal in 1870 with modifications. Philip Schaff called for federal or confederative union in 1893. The first major transconfessional union in North America occurred in 1925 when Canadian Methodists and Presbyterians (some remained in a continuing Presbyterian Church) formed the United Church of Canada. E. Stanley Jones called for union modeled on the U.S. federal-state structure in 1935. The Greenwich Plan of 1949 proposed to unite churches "in sufficient accord in essentials of Christian faith and order" and "already accorded one another mutual recognition of ministers and sacraments." This proposal was distinguished by its inclusion of both historically black and predominantly white churches. In 1957 the Congregational Church and the Evangelical and Reformed Church (itself a merger of Lutheran and Reformed strains) formed the United Church of Christ. Union negotiations between the American Baptist Convention and the Christian Church (Disciples of Christ) and between the Presbyterian Church in the U.S.A. and the Episcopal Church failed.

At the time of the Oberlin conference significant cultural changes were underway. The 1950s are often considered a time of return to normality and the growth of prosperity following the devastation and dislocation of the Second World War, preceded by the Great Depression. Church membership was higher than ever before. Yet much that is associated with turmoil in the 1960s actually originated earlier: new interest in ethnicity and diversity, new attitudes towards sex and the family, and a new feminism. Counter-cultural forces reflected the values of openness and spontaneity and a loose attitude toward morality and society. Margins of the culture began to erode the established center. In the Oberlin report itself we find discussions of racial and economic stratification, population mobility, governmental policies and programs, and diversity.

Despite everything, most Americans retained an overall sense of possibility. People had come here for the opportunity to drop their old lives and remake themselves. After the Holocaust there were reservations, but most were drawn by the openness of the American horizon. Some had a strong sense of the limits imposed on black people, but they rejected any socially deterministic vision and in this sense had a vision of greater openness in society. Church leaders envisioned the churches in the vanguard of social and economic justice.

As the sixties unfolded some cultural influences encouraged theological dissent and open rifts over church teachings and practices. The authority of all established institutions came into question, including denominations and their leaders. Most Christians continued to believe that loyalty to the churches and the following of Christ were mutually supportive and ultimately identical, but others found an irreconcilable conflict between ecclesiastical Christianity and the teachings of the gospel.

In defiance of cultural and social developments, the powerful evangelism of conservative Evangelical, Pentecostal, and Holiness churches began to attract growing numbers of people. These churches were anything but uniform, but their emphasis variously on scriptural infallibility, strict morality, mission areas, tithing, and spiritual experience was compelling. The global ecumenical fellowship would soon expand to include all the Orthodox churches and the Roman Catholic Church. Ecumenism would thrive in the sixties, but the newer American denominations would continue apart, despite efforts of some on each side.

9

Department of Faith and Order Studies

A search began for an executive director of a new department of Faith and Order Studies to be located in the National Council of Churches. It was led by Leila W. Anderson of the National Council and Roswell P. Barnes of the U.S. Conference of the World Council, with the assistance of consultant Keith R. Bridston, secretary of the World Council Commission on Faith and Order. For several months Bridston was in the United States to prepare a report on prospects for the department. William A. Norgren, a priest of the Episcopal Church recently returned from Christ Church, Oxford, was appointed director in May 1959. The department reported to the general board through general secretary Roy G. Ross and the council's policy and strategy committee. James I. McCord, president of Princeton Theological Seminary, accepted chairmanship of a small advisory committee made up of theologians, church leaders, and state and local council secretaries.

With guidance from lay leader Leila Anderson, the first task of the director was to know and become known by church, council, seminary, and student and youth leaders known to be interested. The annual meetings of the Association of Council Secretaries held at the council's Conference Point Camp in Wisconsin offered opportunities to interact with state and local council leaders across the nation. World Council Faith and Order meetings provided connections to theologians and others from churches in other nations. Visits to seminary presidents, heads of churches, denominational ecumenical commissions, and youth and student movements followed.

James McCord and the director met regularly in Princeton to plan advisory committee meetings, which had responsibility for studies and other programs and initiatives. From the outset the committee understood that Oberlin proposed not only studies but also a pattern of regional and local participation. Work would center on theological studies carried out largely, though not exclusively, by national study commissions. Educational programs would seek to increase public awareness of the church's oneness and the obligation to manifest that unity and its urgency for evangelism.

The first national study commission, chaired by Robert T. Handy of

Union Theological Seminary, set to work on The Ecclesiological Significance of Councils of Churches, as requested by Oberlin. At the same time the advisory committee heeded Oberlin's advice that "of all presently existing structures, the councils of churches provide the best and most available vehicle for widespread faith and order studies." Such studies in state and local councils were increasing, but numbers were still small. The Pacific Northwest region, led by Bill Cate of the Portland Council, held a Faith and Order consultation to address the lingering frontier ecclesiastical heritage that was believed to have little appreciation of the corporate nature of the church and a lack of clarity about the relationship of the church to society. In the Pacific Southwest a Faith and Order conference heard from theologians such as Paul Tillich. State conferences were projected in Massachusetts, Ohio, Rhode Island, and Pennsylvania. City councils in the National Capital Area, Staten Island, Boise, and Albany studied various subjects. The director worked with the councils, reported to the annual U.S. Conference of the World Council at Buck Hill Falls, Pennsylvania, and met with representatives of the Canadian Council of Churches and the British Council of Churches.

Advice gleaned from such visits and consultations led the director to suggest extending Faith and Order work to congregations:

> If Christians in each place are to discuss and understand the questions of the faith, the order of the Church, and its worship, in their bearing on unity and renewal, and if they are to discern the significance of the ecumenical movement, then knowledge and information must be accessible, and they must have occasion to meet and discuss. . . .
>
> While the growth of study in each place is of the greatest importance, study cannot in the nature of things be undertaken by all or even most Christian people. . . . The essential oneness of the Church must be proclaimed and understood in each place through additional means. If we look to other ingredients in the Christian life, three enterprises suggest themselves immediately: sustained prayer for unity and for separated communions, rekindling and strengthening of love between Christians now divided, and experience of worship in other Christian traditions. . . .

In the United States the ecumenical movement as a whole has concentrated on the building of *inter*-church social and administrative structures that speak of the goal of unity, and in which some degree of unity can be experienced. . . . While this is unquestionably of the greatest value, it is not enough. As long as Christian people must be drawn out of their congregations and denominational bodies onto neutral ground in order to discover one another, just so long will the ecumenical movement fail to engage all Christian people. . . .

Should we not, in addition to drawing representatives of separated bodies of Christians out of their congregations into inter-denominational association, bring the Faith and Order movement to the people in their congregations? May we not be called in the next phase of the movement to extend participation through the existing *church* social and administrative structures?[12]

When in January 1959, at the conclusion of a prayer service for Christian unity, Pope John XXIII announced his intention to convoke "an ecumenical council for the universal church," much speculation occurred about the implications for other churches. In June 1960 the pope created the Secretariat for Promoting Christian Unity to enable "those who bear the name of Christians but are separated from this apostolic see to find more easily the path by which they may arrive at the unity for which Christ prayed." Cardinal Augustin Bea was appointed its president and Johannes Willebrands the secretary. Among the secretariat's fifteen consultants were Gregory Baum from Canada and Gustave Weigel, S.J., and George Tavard, O.P., from the United States.

Leaders of the council's member churches considered it appropriate to pursue contacts with Roman Catholics known to be open to ecumenism. Accordingly, the director visited Weigel at Woodstock College. Along with John Sheerin, a Paulist, Weigel had actually been

---

12. William A. Norgren, "All in Each Place," *Faith and Order Trends* 1, no. 3 (June 1961): 2-3.

an observer at the Oberlin conference. When asked whether permission should be sought for Roman Catholics to attend ecumenical meetings, Weigel is reported to have answered no, explaining that bishops have difficulty blessing soldiers when they go off to war but no difficulty blessing those who return victorious. Other visits were to George Higgins at the National Catholic Welfare Conference, Charles Angel of the Friars of the Atonement, George Tavard, Bishop John Wright of Pittsburgh, Frs. Dieckman, McDonnell, and Barry at the Benedictine Abbey at Collegeville, Minnesota, and Charles Boyer, S.J., at the International Unitas Association in Rome.

San Francisco: A Turning Point

San Francisco was the location of the National Council's next general assembly in December 1960, the first to have Faith and Order on its agenda. In a remarkable address McCord signaled a turning point for ecumenism in America:

> Faith and Order has to do with the Gospel, with evangelism, with the mission of the Church. It is not an "aside" or an "above." It is central to the Church, and the Church is central to the purpose of God in the world. Moreover, the significance can be seen in widening the base of ecumenical discussion, participation, and concern. It is increasingly clear that the ecumenical movement here and abroad cannot be equated with pan-Protestantism. Eastern Orthodoxy has played and continues to play a major role in all discussions and actions, and is a constant challenge to us to realize the catholicity of our own traditions.
>
> Again, Faith and Order reflects the extent of the theological renewal that has gone on in our churches during and since World War II. This renewal began when biblical and theological scholarship re-discovered the living center of our faith, Jesus Christ, and called us back to Him for renewal and correction and for common participation in His own ministry and mission. Our churches are no longer willing to compare their traditions,

to seek some least common denominator, and to succumb to historical relativism. In acknowledgment of the living center and in awareness of the awful responsibility before Him to the world and for the world, they are responding with a common commitment to seek that form of visible unity that will most clearly manifest Christ's reconciling power to the world. . . .

My theme has been that cooperation is not enough. I say this as one who is profoundly grateful for his own tradition, as well as for what cooperative Christianity has done during the first half of the twentieth century. But it is a luxury now that we can no longer afford. Many sensitive critics are convinced that we have seen the end of the protestant era. In the economy of God it has been allowed four centuries. The situation now is radically changed. Much of the West is admittedly ex-Christian, while in most of the world indigenous younger churches are living in an age that is pre-Christian. They have seen the inadequacy of our old structures and forms and are agonizingly seeking new forms of ecumenical expression and experience. This challenge can be met by nothing less than a willingness on our part to take a radical step forward in our quest for visible, corporate unity that will be an expression of a new indwelling of the Holy Spirit among God's people. . . . We are called to obedience by the same Christ about whom John Calvin asked in his Commentary on Hebrews: "For to what end did Christ come except to collect us all into one body from that dispersion in which we are now wandering. Therefore the nearer His coming, the more we ought to labor that the scattered may be assembled and united together, that there may be one flock and one shepherd."[13]

Lesslie Newbigin, general secretary of the International Missionary Council and a bishop of the united Church of South India, spoke at a crowded lunch event on the theme Breaking the Deadlock Between the Churches:

13. James I. McCord, "Cooperation Is Not Enough," *Trends* 1, no. 2 (February 1961): 1-3, 9.

We are concerned with the truth as it is in Jesus and with the recovery of that integrity of the life of the Church which comes from being in Christ. The value of any ecumenical institution or of any union of churches does not lie in the number of millions of people who are related to one another. It lies in the degree to which, by that institution, there is in some measure a recovery of the integrity in faith and life of the Church, the body of Christ. . . .

The ecumenical movement involves us basically and essentially in what the Amsterdam assembly called "receiving correction one from another," in the painful process of listening to others whose interpretation of the gospel is perhaps repellent and strange to us, and whom we are yet bound to respect and attend to, because we are unable to deny the presence of Christ in their midst.

(Unity in the truth) does not mean that we are concerned with unanimity in verbal statements. These verbal statements are necessary instruments, but not constitutive of the unity with which we are concerned. . . . We do not find in the New Testament that the Lord first proposed a system of belief and then invited those who were willing to subscribe to it to form themselves into an association. He began by drawing men to Himself, He who is the truth. His word was first "Follow me," then "Learn of me," and finally "I am the way, the truth and the life." Our unity is in Him, an engrafting into one body, a regeneration which involves the reorientation of our whole being towards Him and therefore — in Him — towards one another, a total commitment to one reconciled fellowship. Here we come to our area of deepest perplexity. It is so hard for us to know the form of the one Body in this complex twentieth century civilization of ours.[14]

Newbigin appealed for study of a new description of visible unity approved unanimously by the World Council Commission on Faith and

---

14. Lesslie Newbigin, "The Truth as It Is in Jesus," *Trends* 1, no. 2 (February 1961): 4-6.

Order at St. Andrews, Scotland, for transmission to the next assembly of the World Council at New Delhi in 1961.

In a sermon at San Francisco's Grace Cathedral immediately before the National Council assembly, Eugene Carson Blake, chief executive officer of the United Presbyterian Church, proposed that the Episcopal Church together with the United Presbyterian Church invite the Methodist Church and the United Church of Christ to form a plan of church union. The bold proposal called for the reconciliation of churches of Catholic tradition with churches of Reformed, Protestant, and Evangelical traditions. Blake specified that the plan should "have within it the kind of broad and deep agreement which gives promise of much wider union than seems possible at the present moment, looking ultimately to the reunion of the whole of Christ's Church."

Principles of reunion important to the Catholic tradition were outlined: "The reunited Church must have visible and historical continuity with the Church of all ages before and after the Reformation . . . without adopting any particular theory of historic succession, the reunited Church shall provide at its inception for the consecration of all its bishops by bishops and presbyters both in the apostolic succession and out of it from all over the world from all Christian churches which would authorize or permit them to take part." It should "clearly confess the historic trinitarian faith received from the Apostles and set forth in the Apostles' and Nicene Creeds." It would "administer the two sacraments, instituted by Christ . . ." these being "understood truly as Means of Grace by which God's Grace and presence are made available to His people."

Principles of reunion important to the Reformation tradition included "continuing reformation under the Word of God by the guidance of the Holy Spirit." A "truly democratic" system of government would be required, "recognizing that the whole people of God are Christ's Church, that all Christians are Christ's ministers even though some in the church are separated and ordained to the ministry of word and sacrament." Also, "the reunited church must find a way to include within its catholicity (and because of it) a wide diversity of theological formulations of the faith and a variety of worship and liturgy including worship that is non-liturgical."

The Blake proposal elicited wide interest. The General Convention of the Episcopal Church accepted it in 1961, as did the three other churches. Acceptances also came from the Christian Church (Disciples of Christ), the three historically black Methodist churches — African Methodist Episcopal, African Methodist Episcopal Zion, and Christian Methodist Episcopal — and the International Council of Community Churches.

Representatives of these churches formed the Consultation on Church Union. Over many years the consultation would struggle with theological issues involved in Blake's vision and the form such union should assume in the United States. Observers from Roman Catholic, Lutheran, and other churches attended meetings of the consultation. A Methodist theologian was heard to observe that while the Episcopalians represented the Catholic majority in the world, in the consultation they were a minority. In the wider ecumenical movement, however, participation of churches in the Catholic tradition was expanding.

New Delhi: Unity and the Orthodox

The third assembly of the World Council of Churches gathered at New Delhi in 1961. Here the separate International Missionary Council merged with the World Council, thus uniting the missionary stream of the ecumenical movement with the Life and Work and Faith and Order streams. Here also the Orthodox churches living in communist nations joined the council. The Ecumenical Patriarchate and several other Orthodox churches were, of course, founding members. Now the Russian Orthodox Church became the council's largest member church, accompanied by the Bulgarian, Polish, and Romanian Orthodox churches (the Georgian Orthodox Church joined in 1962). In a time of "cold war" between the U.S.S.R. and the West the accession of Orthodox churches was a remarkable witness to the unity of Christians across political divisions. In the United States, however, not all Christians welcomed the exchanges of U.S. and U.S.S.R. church leaders that were arranged by the National Council. Orthodox churches in America maintained ties with their mother churches in Europe and the

Middle East, but, led by Archbishop Iakovos of the Greek Orthodox Archdiocese, they also formed a Standing Conference of Canonical Orthodox Bishops in the Americas.

Two Pentecostal churches, a tradition that had not previously participated, were admitted to membership of the World Council, as were seventeen Protestant and Anglican churches. Still, many of the world's churches were not at New Delhi. For the first time, however, the Roman Catholic Church was officially present at an assembly with five Vatican-appointed observers.

Additional churches brought new vitality to the ecumenical movement but also greater complexity. It was becoming important to formulate a shared goal. Building on decades of discussions in Faith and Order, New Delhi approved a description of the goal of visible unity in three paragraphs.[15]

The first states, in part, "The love of the Father and the Son in the unity of the Holy Spirit is the source and goal of the unity which the Triune God wills for all men and creation. We believe that we share in this unity in the Church of Jesus Christ. . . . In him alone, given by the Father to be the Head of the Body, the Church has its true unity. . . ."

The second states, "the unity which is both God's will and his gift to his Church is being made visible as all in each place who are baptized into Jesus Christ and confess him as Lord and Savior are brought by the Holy Spirit into one fully committed fellowship. . . ." Elements of unity are "holding the one apostolic faith, preaching the one Gospel, breaking the one bread, joining in common prayer, and having a corporate life reaching out in witness and service to all." This unity means that all "at the same time are united with the whole Christian fellowship in all places and all ages in such wise that ministry and members are accepted by all, and that all can act and speak together as occasion requires for the tasks to which God calls his people."

The third paragraph allows that this brief description leaves many questions unanswered, but states that "unity does not imply simply uniformity of organization, rite or expression."

15. W. A. Visser 't Hooft, ed., *The New Delhi Report* (New York: Association Press, 1962), pp. 116-22.

A commentary appended to the statement explains that the word "place" is used "both in its primary sense of local neighborhood and also, under modern conditions of other areas in which Christians need to express unity in Christ . . . each school where they study, in each factory or office where they work and in each congregation where they worship, as well as between congregations. . . ." It is also used of "wider geographical areas such as states, provinces or nations, and certainly refers to all Christian people in each place regardless of race."

Ecumenists celebrated the New Delhi statement. It opened new vistas and energy for the movement. The main criticism was that its strong emphasis on unity in each place allowed insufficient attention to the unity of all in every place.

Montreal: Unity and Complexedness

The fourth World Conference on Faith and Order met in 1963 at Montreal among fast-moving events. A large Orthodox representation attended. The Second Vatican Council had begun. Biblical scholars and theologians contributed new perspectives that could not be ignored. Representatives of the churches of Asia, Africa, Latin America, and the Caribbean were present in larger numbers than ever before.

Six regions of the world had been asked to prepare reports on their distinctive Faith and Order issues. A North American consultation at Buck Hill Falls received the views of informal Canadian and the U.S. groups. Issues that had been identified at Oberlin six years before were reviewed. The consultation's eleven-page report describes North American Christianity, like North America itself, as an enormously varied phenomenon:

An unparalleled multiplicity of Christian bodies exists, many of which are indistinguishable from one another on theological grounds. American Christianity tends to reflect American culture and to espouse American values, so that churches are often distinguished only with difficulty from the society in which they are set. Hence in North America there is need not only of a clear Christian picture of the Church, but also a clear Christian picture of the world. . . . In speaking of the unity of the Church we are ipso facto speaking of the unity of humanity.[16]

The report applies this analysis to situations of racial separation, class conflict, and international tension. It seems also to be the first North American Faith and Order document to speak of the vocation of women in the church, including the question of ordination. Concerning church union, it suggested that the problem in America of the potential "bigness" of a church union may be addressed by the twin effects of denominational decentralization and of international involvement.

At Montreal the delegates received the final reports from the four European and North American theological commissions that had been meeting following the previous world conference at Lund. There were papers on the ordination of women from Reformed, Anglican, and Orthodox theologians. Biblical scholars Raymond E. Brown from the United States and Ernst Käsemann from Germany presented differing positions on the church in the New Testament. Paul Minear, now director of World Council Faith and Order, coordinated the conference.

Members of the five conference sections debated many issues but registered conclusions on few. The section on Scripture, Tradition, and Traditions did reach a large measure of agreement that would help later discussions about authority in the church. The conference reached common understandings of worship thanks to the liturgical movement, and recommended there be frequent celebrations of Holy Communion. It recognized that a recovery of biblical teaching concerning the royal priesthood of the whole people of God provided the setting of the ordained ministry. It recommended that in future studies a more fully Trinitarian method be followed. And the conviction took hold that the church was challenged to show forth its unity, not only in communion with God in Jesus Christ, but also in discerning God's continuing disclosure in present events, looking for possibilities of proclaiming the gospel and ministering in the world. It spoke to local

16. "Faith and Order Issues in North America," *Trends* 3, no. 3 (June 1963): 1-11.

churches about their ecumenical responsibilities and to denominations about theirs. Finally, its theological affirmation of the eucharistic foundation of unity should not be overlooked:

> Organizational structures will always be necessary; at the same time we affirm that the unity of the Church is to be found not only in the merger of denominational structures but even more profoundly in the koinonia of true eucharistic worship, where the whole Catholic Church is manifest.[17]

Dialogue had grown more difficult — and more necessary — as the ecumenical situation had become more diversified and complex. At the same time, it was seen that the search for unity could make diversity a source of enrichment rather than confessional conflict. After the "promising chaos" of Montreal, Faith and Order set itself the task of developing new methods of dialogue and study as well as preparing a much wider participation in its work. It would be three decades before there would be another world conference on Faith and Order, after substantial progress had been made in the commission.

Second Vatican Council: Unity and Renewal

Pope John XXIII set pastoral norms for the Second Vatican Council during his inaugural discourse in 1962. While holding fast to "the sacred patrimony of truth received from the Fathers," the church must "ever look to the present, to the new conditions and new forms of life introduced into the modern world which have opened new avenues to the Catholic apostolate." He called for reformulation of doctrine where necessary for pastoral effectiveness. And he declared it was the duty of the Catholic Church to work actively that "there may be fulfilled the great mystery of that unity which Jesus Christ invoked with fervent prayer."

17. P. C. Rodger and Lukas Vischer, eds., *The Fourth World Conference on Faith and Order* (New York: Association Press, 1964), p. 46.

Renewal began with reflection on the liturgy and the preparation of a Constitution on the Sacred Liturgy. The observers from other churches appreciated the widened use of Scripture, renewal of preaching, full and active participation of the laity, stress on the communion of the people, and use of the vernacular.

Following the first council session, Cardinal Bea met in New York City with Franklin Clark Fry, president of the United Lutheran Church and chairman of the World Council central committee, and other U.S. leaders. At this discussion of relationships the National Council director of Faith and Order was present. Soon an invitation arrived for him to attend the council as a guest of the secretariat "because of your continuing promotion of the cause of Christian unity."

During council sessions the official observers and guests met weekly with the committee of the Secretariat for Promoting Christian Unity, where they shared positive criticisms, suggestions, and desires about each schema under discussion. The secretariat brought these points to the appropriate council commissions. So it can be said that the dialogue actually began at the council. During plenary sessions, the presence of the observers in a central position by the altar in St. Peter's Basilica continually compelled the attention of council fathers to the question of Christian unity. The council's intention was less to make "progressive" in contrast to "conservative" doctrinal pronouncements on Christian unity and more to leave the door open. The observers, who found much in Roman Catholic theology to which they could not assent, felt that this policy offered hope because it allowed full scope to the dialogue that lay ahead.

After the death of Pope John, Paul VI affirmed the pastoral norms and outlined four objectives in his address to the second session in 1963: "the knowledge, or, if you like, the awareness of the church, its renewal, the bringing together of all Christians in unity, the dialogue of the church with the contemporary world." Catholic laymen were admitted to the council as auditors, whose advice could be sought by council commissions. Soon they were joined by what are believed to be the first women in history to participate in an ecumenical council.

The second session was dominated by vigorous disputation on the theme of the church and formulation of the Dogmatic Constitution on the Church. The observers were impressed by the biblical and historical content of the constitution, but were aware that time would be required for its teachings to be embodied in the consciousness of people in dioceses and parishes. This constitution and the later Decree on Ecumenism were the most significant enactments of the council from an ecumenical perspective. Other constitutions, decrees, and declarations adopted at the second, third, and fourth sessions dealt, for the most part, either with particular sections or elements within the church, or with activities or relationships of the church vis-à-vis other religions. The Constitution on Divine Revelation left open the question of the precise relation of scripture and tradition, but affirmed one source of revelation, the gospel, which is the revelation of God.

The Decree on Ecumenism lays down principles of Catholic ecumenism. The relation of the separated churches is defined: "For men who believe in Christ and have been properly baptized are brought into a certain, though imperfect, communion with the Catholic Church . . . all those justified through baptism are incorporated into Christ." While "the separated churches and communities" are understood to be deficient in certain respects, they "have by no means been deprived of significance and importance in the mystery of salvation . . . the Spirit of Christ has not refrained from using them as means of salvation which derive their effectiveness from the very fullness of grace and truth entrusted to the Catholic Church."

Previously the Roman Catholic Church conceived reunion as the return of the separated communities to the authority of Rome. Reunion was now visualized as a movement by all towards a common aim. The council allowed that past disagreements had been due to developments for which "at times men of both sides were to blame" and called for study and dialogue "on an equal footing" in a spirit of charity. This profound change opened unprecedented possibilities. During and following the council the observers often joined Roman Catholic bishops and theologians in explaining its decisions on television and radio and in print and public meetings.

National and Local Effects

Over the first five years National Council Faith and Order carried out a program of studies, but much of its effort went into education and stimulation of regional and local studies and dialogue. The Second Vatican Council engaged the interest of member churches and its decisions led to changes designed to help Roman Catholics contribute to the ecumenical movement. Even before the council began, Faith and Order presented a paper to the National Council policy and strategy committee titled The Roman Catholic Church and the Ecumenical Movement. The paper recognized the fluidity of thought about ecumenism in that church and recommended thoughtfulness and wise and timely action. The general board noted "with great satisfaction increasing evidence of warmer relations with the Roman Catholic Church in many parts of the world . . . [and] welcomes the prospect that these warmer relations will be increasingly reflected in the life of the churches in the United States."

Already archdioceses in Baltimore, Boston, and elsewhere were appointing ecumenical committees. An Orthodox-Protestant-Roman Catholic dialogue group in Portland, Oregon, was the first to be organized by a city council Faith and Order commission. Catholic-Protestant meetings and dialogues proliferated but still lagged behind Europe. A survey of National Council staff showed a remarkable number of contacts with Catholic individuals and organizations as well as some cooperative work, almost all of a Life and Work type. The creation in 1964 of the Bishops Committee for Ecumenical Affairs, headed by Cardinal Lawrence G. Shehan of Baltimore with Monsignor William W. Baum as executive secretary, provided a national Roman Catholic center for Christian unity, making possible official relations with the council and its member churches.

Prayer for Christian unity was a priority. Vatican II stimulated a sharp increase in prayer, but a problem remained. In 1908 a Chair of Unity Octave was created in the United States by Paul James Francis, founder of the Fathers of the Atonement, Graymoor. It was observed in the week preceding the January feast of the Conversion of St. Paul with the intention of the "return of all separated Churches to the Holy See." The French Abbé Paul Couturier recognized in the 1930s that the octave could not be widely accepted by other Christians and urged acceptance of a new intention "that the unity of all Christians may come, such as Christ wills and by the means he wills." World Council Faith and Order, which had long sponsored prayer for unity at Pentecost, advocated a January observance to coincide with that of Couturier. In 1964 the two began to use the same prayer leaflet. Consultation in the United States between National Council Faith and Order, the Bishops' Committee, and Graymoor led to a Week of Prayer for Christian Unity in January sponsored by all three. By 1966 more than 1,367,000 leaflets were being distributed each year by Graymoor and the World Council office in the United States.

A consultation on the theology of prayer for unity and pastoral considerations was sponsored by World Council Faith and Order with the participation of the Vatican secretariat. Its report proposed giving greater prominence to thanksgiving for the degree of unity already achieved, and stressed the necessity of increased cooperation "to serve the needs of men and society" and the desirability of adaptations of the internationally prepared leaflet to the varying regional situations. Adaptation in the United States became the joint responsibility of Faith and Order and Graymoor. National Council Faith and Order also took over sponsorship of World-Wide Communion Sunday, an observance mainly among Protestants on the first Sunday in October.

The idea for Living Room Dialogues came from William B. Greenspun, director of the Roman Catholic Confraternity of Christian Doctrine. He envisioned a resource book for laypeople to be used by Protestant, Catholic, and Orthodox friends and neighbors. Greenspun and the director edited a collection of prayers, Bible readings, and other resources from pairs of Catholic and Protestant authors. The suggestion was that dialogue groups meet once a month for seven months. Published in 1965 by Paulist Press and the National Council, *Living Room Dialogues* was recommended to local councils of churches and diocesan leaders of the confraternity. Groups were organized by councils, ministerial associations, women's and men's organizations, and local churches. Clergy were expected to help initiate the dialogues and serve as consultants but not to participate in the sessions so that laity might speak freely, openly, and without embarrassment.

Public response was phenomenal. A *Second Living Room Dialogues,* edited by Greenspun and Cynthia Wedel appeared in 1967 and a *Third Living Room Dialogues* by James J. Yound in 1970.

Other signs of movement appeared. The archdiocese of Santa Fe became a member of the New Mexico Council of Churches. A Texas Conference of Churches was formed by the Roman Catholic dioceses of Texas and the Texas Council of Churches. Archbishop James P. Davis of Santa Fe gave his opinion that, while some differences on certain policies of the state council would certainly occur, the archdiocese would state the differences and act accordingly, while working together wherever it was possible to do so. The first Catholic parishes became members of councils in Tulsa and Grand Rapids. Priests joined ministerial associations in many places.

A Joint Working Group of representatives from the National Council and the Bishops' Committee, led by John Coventry Smith and Archbishop John J. Carberry of St. Louis, met from 1965 to 1971 to consider relations between the Catholic Church and councils of churches, mixed marriages, education, cooperation for peace, justice, and development, and dialogue with the Jews. The group formulated recommendations to the Vatican secretariat regarding the issue of conditional baptism of converts to the Roman Catholic Church. Staff responsibility for the Joint Working Group was shared by William Baum, the director, and staff colleagues.

Work with the National Council took a major step forward in 1966 when, with the advice of Baum of the Bishops' Committee, David J. Bowman, S.J., was seconded to the staff of Faith and Order by the Society of Jesus. At this time the general board voted to include the Roman Catholic Church in the list of nonmember churches in agreement with the preamble to the constitution, making it possible for it to participate in council program units.

Councils, Churches, and Unity

We have already noted that councils of churches as agencies of cooperation proliferated in twentieth-century America. More than a thousand had come into being in states and localities. In mid-century in-creased interest in the doctrine of the church influenced congregations and jurisdictions of communions that were members of the councils. The Oberlin conference called for a "study of the ecclesiological signif-icance of local, state, and national councils of churches." A National Council Faith and Order study commission submitted a report on the subject to the general board in 1963.[18]

The report traces the conciliar motif from the early church coun-cils and synods to the reformatory councils of the fourteenth and fif-teenth centuries. Councils of churches are seen as more nearly like the reformatory councils in their attempt to reconcile the estranged east-ern and western churches and to overcome the "great schism" in the western church, but with significant differences. A survey taken of the state and local councils showed that the communions had not dealt significantly with theological or ecclesiological questions in the forma-tion or operation of the councils, yet the existence of the councils actu-ally presupposed a high degree of mutual recognition.

On the understanding that "councils of churches can be said to have ecclesiological significance if they bear significantly the marks of the Church in important ways," an affirmative answer is given to the question, "Is the reality of the Church expressed in councils of churches?" Convincing signs of the presence and activity of the Holy Spirit can be found in the councils movement, although the commis-sion is careful to point out that, because the Holy Spirit moves where it wills, it does not logically follow from such presence that a visible church is brought into being.

"Another way in which the reality of the church is expressed in councils of churches is their provision of structures through which the denominations may participate in loving service, *diakonia,* that is es-sential to the fullness of the Church." Councils also "can serve as par-tial expressions of the general ministry of the whole church in effective

18. *The Ecclesiological Significance of Councils of Churches: A Working Paper Pre-pared by the National Study Commission on the Ecclesiological Significance of Coun-cils of Churches* (New York: National Council of Churches, 1963). Reprinted in Jo-seph A. Burgess and Jeffrey Gros, eds., *Growing Consensus I: Church Dialogues in the United States, 1962-1991* (New York: Paulist Press, 1995), pp. 581-613.

ways. The general ministry, as carried through the councils, does not supplant the special ordained ministry of the churches nor does it represent an emerging new form of that ministry, but it serves as an effective reminder and token that the ministry of Christ is one despite the brokenness of the Church."

In councils not only denominations but also "their members are brought into an intimate and sometimes profound relationship with one another in which together they witness to a larger and more inclusive community than exists in any separate church or denomination." But although "the reality of the Church is expressed in certain ways in councils of churches, they do not normally have creeds or determine theological issues, and do not administer the sacrament or ordain."

A second question is asked: "Are councils of churches instruments which the churches should use in fulfilling their mission?" "In separation from one another, the denominations can lose sight of important emphases of the Gospel," and in competition with each other "they can magnify certain duties and practices but let others go in an effort to maintain distinctiveness." The councils can help "to bring the churches into encounter so that they must witness to each other of what they deem essential to the faith . . . in the mutual and free search for fuller understanding of Christ and His Church." Councils can also assist the denominations to advance the mission and evangelistic tasks of the church by eliminating duplication of effort and sharing information.

The third question is, "Are councils contributing to the unity of the Church?" The councils are ". . . improvisations made necessary because of the divided status of the churches. They are expedients, divinely guided, many of us believe, but provisional. They stand in the prophetic tradition, called into being for a particular function at a particular time for a particular need. Councils of churches are catalysts for the reunion of churches; though they may not invade the freedom of communions and make their unitive decisions for them, they can and should invade the consciences of the denominations in the name of the One Lord and press them to add to cooperative service, serious concern for union."

The report remarks, "As they press the ecclesiological question, the councils of churches cannot expect to remain unchanged themselves." Yet, "the prospect of the self-transcendence of denominations and councils of churches by structures which far more fully manifest the unity of the Church is not a cause for regret but for rejoicing."

The advisory committee recommended and the general board voted to recommend to member communions that they study the report and the way the churches relate to each other, and that both councils and denominations establish committees and offices for such study. Councils of churches were already taking on Faith and Order work, but the study commission's report was curiously silent about an important initiative of certain denominations — the creating of ecumenical offices to oversee and promote relations, not only through councils but also directly with other communions.

Order and Organization

Oberlin suggested another study, "an ongoing deliberative theological study in the area of order and organization." One Oberlin preparatory group had asked whether there are criteria for a distinction between an "ordered structure which at all times and in all places serves as the means by which God constitutes the Church as the Church and an organization which under particular circumstances gives effective expression to some aspect or another of the primary structure."[19] In 1963 the Faith and Order advisory committee appointed a national study commission on Order and Organization led by Jerald C. Brauer of the University of Chicago Divinity School. Its first meeting agreed to approach the question of order through the question of organization or, put another way, through an investigation of what actually goes on in the life and activities of congregations and other ecclesiastical organizations. The feeling was that departure from traditional approaches might open up the stalemate over the doctrine of the church and make a particular American contribution to the ecumenical conversation. A research project was begun.

The second meeting decided that the commission itself might carry

19. Minear, *Nature,* pp. 210-11.

out the investigation through two subgroups. The first was assigned the task of formulating theological norms for an empirical investigation of the church, but the group decided the commission had made a fruitful decision at the first meeting and the decision of its second meeting could not be implemented.

The third meeting of the commission in 1965 received a substantial report on American church organization from the research project assistant guided by member Gibson Winter. It proposed to continue examining the data, prepare a summary, and then outline any future work as needed.

Meanwhile the World Council Commission on Faith and Order, meeting at Aarhus in 1964, sensed the importance of the topic and initiated a study on Spirit, Order, and Organization. Plans were built in part upon the work of the National Council study, so the latter can be said to have made a contribution through both its insights and difficulties. Gibson Winter prepared a memorandum of advice to the World Council. The U.S. commission was discharged in 1968. No report was written, but some papers and research documents were published.[20]

Communicatio in Sacris

Communicatio in Sacris — Communication in Holy Things — was the subject for a working group begun in 1965 and led by Lewis S. Mudge of the Presbyterian Church. The task was to look at instances of sharing by Christians in worship of churches not their own, including the long-debated question of intercommunion. The practice of Communicatio in Sacris was largely a matter of local initiative; denominational legislatures took very little initiative. Local decisions were made on the basis of the local situation, not simply on formal theological principles. Such decisions presupposed a sharing of Christian life, or more precisely study and action leading to and from the act of joint worship.

20. Gibson Winter, Religious Identity (New York: Macmillan, 1968). Paul M. Van Buren, "What Do We Mean by an 'Empirical Investigation of the Church'?" in Theological Explorations (London: SCM Press, 1968).

The church's mission was involved; indeed, the action of joint worship can be understood as an act of mission.

An inquiry of a cross-section of communions in the United States showed the majority had no official statements on intercommunion, probably due to a strong tendency toward congregational autonomy, but they were able to point to historic positions or at least to describe customary practices in congregations. Three groups of communions were identified: (1) those in which, except for certain very limited restrictions, it is customary to invite all who wish to receive the eucharist and to allow their members to participate in the eucharist of other communions; (2) those in which the normative practice is to limit reception of the eucharist to their own members and not to allow their members to receive the eucharist of other communions, but allow exceptions under certain specified conditions; (3) those that, save in very exceptional circumstances, restrict their eucharist to their own members and do not permit them to receive the eucharist of other communions. Contrary to popular opinion, there were not just two policy options, open and closed communion, but a range of possibilities.

Case studies followed — of large ecumenical conferences, student meetings, retreats, study conferences, civil rights and war protests, the armed forces, national parks, parish cooperation and community churches, colleges and universities. The working group also met with representatives of a new planned community named Columbia in Maryland.

The group's report includes theological reflections on *communicatio in humanum*, the world in eschatological perspective, and the doctrine of intention. Written in popular style by Mudge, the report appears in the book *The Crumbling Walls*.[21]

More Projects

A consultation in 1965 with representatives of the Church of the New Jerusalem (Swedenborgian) explored its history and faith, particularly

---

21. Lewis Mudge, *The Crumbling Walls* (Philadelphia: Westminster Press, 1970).

its Christology, beliefs concerning the Trinity, and eschatology. Later the church (not to be confused with the Swedenborgian Church) applied and was accepted as a member church of the National Council. Consultations were held with Seventh Day Adventists in 1969 and 1970 at the request of the World Council, but no action followed.

Project New York was an experimental panel of local city pastors working with Faith and Order in 1969 and 1970 to uncover new modes for local studies. It had been proving easier to adapt the Faith and Order pattern to small or middle-sized urban areas than to great centers of population. Because of intense demands on the time of people in the metropolis it proved difficult to maintain continuity of personnel in this project. It became clear that any large united church would have to structure greater diversity in its life and work in a large city far beyond what existing denominational patterns would allow. Church union could not mean simply incorporating people into one unit; openness to new forms would be required. The project ended with a question: how to build a Faith and Order unit in New York City. The answer was to build it into an urban mission consortium then being proposed.

The Eucharist and the Ecumenical Movement was led by Harry J. McSorley, C.S.P., of the Roman Catholic Church. Two sessions of the group in 1970 produced a report on The Eucharist in the Life of the Church: An Ecumenical Consensus, which was printed in no fewer than three journals.[22] The report brought together and rephrased achievements of dialogues on the eucharist. Participants spanned Catholic, Disciples of Christ, Episcopal, Lutheran, Methodist, Orthodox, Presbyterian, and Southern Baptist traditions. A Quaker participant joined with some hesitation, and the experience suggested that further dialogue between sacramental Christians and Quakers could be fruitful. The report was submitted to the Vatican secretariat, which responded positively. Plans were made to explore ways the churches might move ahead in light of the emerging consensus, and the central-

22. "The Eucharist in the Life of the Church: An Ecumenical Consensus," *The Ecumenist* 8, no. 6 (September-October 1970): 89-93; *The American Ecclesiastical Review* (February 1971), Comments (June 1971); *Ecumenical Trends* 1, no. 11 (February 1973). Comments in *St. Vladimir's Theological Quarterly* 15, nos. 1-2 (1971).

ity of the eucharist in Christian worship. The project was terminated in 1972 because of financial difficulties after a report emphasizing that Christians could now abandon past polemical categories when speaking about the eucharist.

The National Faith and Order Colloquium

As early as 1964 the director reported to the advisory committee that "Faith and Order is now established and to a degree understood in U.S. ecumenical circles beyond the corps of Faith and Order specialists. What we must do now is to exercise leadership through information and ideas." At the time, the National Council was undergoing the first of what would be many restructures. One of the results was a renamed Commission on Faith and Order with increased representation and a Department of Faith and Order located in a new Division of Christian Unity, headed by Cynthia Wedel of the Episcopal Church and assisted by Robert C. Dodds of the United Church of Christ. The priority for Faith and Order became the planning of a wider national body of representatives from member as well as nonmember churches to be the central instrument for Faith and Order dialogue in the United States. Although sponsored by the department, the National Faith and Order Colloquium would be independent of council structures so that persons from churches outside the council might participate freely. Summaries of the colloquium's studies and discussions would be made available to the churches, the Faith and Order commission, and others. The list of nonmember churches began with the American Lutheran Church, the Church of God (Anderson, Indiana), the Lutheran Church–Missouri Synod, and the Roman Catholic Church. Southern Baptists also participated, but as individuals. The National Council's member Protestant, Orthodox, and Episcopal churches completed this wider circle.

The Meanings and Practices of Conversion was the topic of the historic first National Faith and Order Colloquium, meeting at a Chicago hotel from June 12 to 17, 1966. James I. McCord was elected chair and Albert C. Outler, Alexander Schmemann, and Bishop James P.

Shannon vice-chairs. The topic presented itself as an ecumenical problem. Across the centuries there had remained some basic, undefined notion of turning to God, which might be identified as a tradition of conversion, mixed with many historically conditioned traditions about it. Selected positions illustrated this: Clement of Alexandria as one who lived in an ancient pagan milieu, Martin Luther as one whose life may or may not be called an example of conversion, August Hermann Franke as an influence on pietism, John Wesley as the beginner of a religious movement, John Henry Newman as one whose life was a process of change ending in the Roman Catholic Church, and Charles G. Finney as one who developed many of the evangelistic methods of the nineteenth century. Philosopher John Edwin Smith was asked to help with the analysis, because the term "conversion" has many meanings.

After the problematic was clarified, the colloquium was ready to hear afresh the biblical witness associated with the event of turning to God and God's people. The Bible refuses to be heard in a vacuum. Its voice comes in the midst of a variety of ideologies, mass media, manipulative techniques, and the collectivism of conformity. Papers were presented on proselytism, contemporary practices of conversion, and social-scientific perspectives. Selected papers and discussion materials were published in *Mid-Stream* for individuals and study groups.[23]

The topic for the next colloquium arose in the discussions: What is the content and shape of the church's evangel by which and to which it seeks the conversion of humankind?

Evangelism in a Pluralistic Society

The second colloquium was at Notre Dame University in 1967. In a historical introduction, Robert T. Handy showed how we arrived at the present condition of religious pluralism in the United States. David O. Moberg set out a sociological profile of contemporary evangelism practices. A collection of statements from denominational evan-

23. William A. Norgren, ed., "The Meanings and Practices of Conversion," *Mid-Stream* 8, no. 3 (1969).

gelism secretaries was provided, and people from the field were present to provide material out of their experience and conviction.

Attention shifted to the character of the world to be evangelized and its implications for evangelism. Joseph P. Fitzpatrick, S.J., offered a scientific description of pluralism as it exists in the United States. Walter J. Ong, S.J., identified alterations being worked by mass communication. Psychologist Ernest van den Haag spoke to the negative role played by evangelism in a pluralist society as seen by a nonchurchman.

The colloquium pressed back to the biblical mandate to evangelize. Addresses from Gordon W. MacRae, S.J., Walter J. Harrelson, and Robert G. Stephanopoulos reminded the colloquium that not all the pluralism is in the society.

Colin W. Williams asked how the ecumenical movement can be put to evangelical service. The church is beginning to realize that it needs to evangelize on an ecumenical basis, but there are strong tensions over how this is to be accomplished. Two polarized religious attitudes have developed: social activists and personal conversionists. Williams said the latter attitude "must be recognized as a temporal or time aspect, where God is calling the individual to respond in a moment. This ignores the entire culture and eliminates the cosmos version — the mission of God in its totality to bring the cultures of the world into the fellowship of Christianity." Although "personal conversion is the driving force of the Christian, it is not enough. It must be related to the total cosmos." He proposed that representatives of both attitudes be brought together to deal with strategy on specific issues and only then reflect theologically on them.

David Hubbard of Fuller Theological Seminary described thought about evangelism in the conservative evangelical wing of Christianity. He urged liberal churches to keep an open mind with respect to evangelical views and not to close the door on such discussions. Evangelicals are moving toward greater concern for social action, but he disputed the idea that heavy emphasis on social action is a form of evangelism.[24]

---

24. William A. Norgren, ed., "Evangelism in a Pluralistic Society," *Mid-Stream* 8, no. 4 (1969).

The underlying question that emerged at this colloquium was the soteriological one: What is the salvation of which the Christian church is both witness and agent?

Salvation and Life

Meeting again in 1968 at Notre Dame, the third colloquium attempted a closer analysis of the question both in terms of definition and the range of agreement and disagreement. In the interim several universities and seminaries arranged seminars, composed of scholars in various fields, to prepare documents on four aspects of the salvation theme: (1) salvation in cosmic dimension, (2) salvation as experienced, (3) time and salvation, (4) man's and God's part in salvation. At the colloquium four working papers emerged from the discussions, repeating the polarities already isolated in 1967 but in greater detail and with more fully developed rationale. These would furnish a structure for the next colloquium.[25]

The fourth colloquium met in 1969 at Concordia Seminary in St. Louis, attended by one hundred theologians, church leaders, and students. Moving from analysis to constructive exposition and application, the task was to prepare a "statement of findings on the meaning of Christian salvation and its relationship to man's life as one basis upon which the churches can evaluate possible strategies in evangelism and mission." John B. Cobb Jr. of the School of Theology at Claremont and Donald E. Miller of Bethany Theological Seminary critiqued the working papers prepared the year before.

Among prepared commentators on Cobb's critique were James Perkins of the Core Experimental Program at Union Theological Seminary; Daniel Olney from a seminar at Catholic University; Wilfred Cantwell Smith of the Center for the Study of World Religions at Harvard University; Steven Matthysse from Pitzer College; and Kenneth L. Schmitz of the School of Philosophy at Catholic University. Commentators on Miller's critique were John William Louis Jr. of Bethany Sem-

25. "Colloquium Quotes," *Unity Trends* 1, no. 17 (1968): 5-10.

inary; James W. Kuhn, senior staff economist of the Council of Economic Advisors in Washington; and Paul W. Pruyser of the Department of Education at the Menninger Foundation and Humanities Department of Stanford University.

A Findings Committee led by Richard Jungkuntz of the Lutheran Church–Missouri Synod presented a draft statement on Salvation and Life for criticism and revision. The colloquium members then voted to make it "their own" and offer it to the churches.[26] It is remarkable that representatives from such diverse communions were able to produce a consensus statement with challenging questions about contemporary evangelism. Since the findings are really the product of four successive colloquia, and the questions are still asked in and between denominations, the statement on Salvation and Life (shorn of its introduction) is printed in an appendix at the end of the present volume.

Salvation and Community

Following the affirmation of the communal dimension in the statement on Salvation and Life, the fifth colloquium took up the theme Salvation and Community in 1970 at Christian Theological Seminary. The focus was on problems threatening to disrupt forms of human community.

Avery Dulles, S.J., presented a paper on The Limits of Authority and Diversity in Christian Unity, which explored the circumstances under which authority is necessary to the cohesion of a community compared to those under which authority stifles the diversity necessary to true community. Willis Elliott presented a paper on Stability and Conflict, which examined when conflict is necessary to the health of a community and when and in what forms it spells the death of community.

Student seminars had already studied the two papers during the spring term just before the colloquium and prepared four draft reports from the perspectives of Polity, Doctrine, Ethics, and Worship. At the

---

26. "Findings of the National Faith and Order Colloquium on 'Salvation and Life,'" *Unity Trends* 2, no. 16 (July 1969): 6-10.

colloquium a small group was asked to observe what authorities were appealed to in the course of discussion. The final reports from the colloquium on Polity, Doctrine, Ethics, and Worship, and the Dulles and Willis papers are preserved in the archives. The colloquium was then recessed in view of a proposed second North American Conference on Faith and Order (see below).

Church Unions and Bilateral Dialogues

Since the 1957 Oberlin conference, five church unions had occurred between communions of the same tradition or confession. Three Presbyterian churches formed the Presbyterian Church in the United States of America, bringing to an end in part effects of the Civil War. Three Lutheran churches (joined by a fourth later) formed the American Lutheran Church. Another four Lutheran churches formed the Lutheran Church in America. Both these unions brought to an end in part effects of European national origins. The two resulting Lutheran churches plus the Lutheran Church–Missouri Synod and the Synod of Evangelical Lutheran Churches formed the National Lutheran Council, which produced a common hymnal and liturgy, but the issue of intercommunion was not resolved. The Methodist Church and the Evangelical United Brethren formed the United Methodist Church. This union resulted in the desegregation of the all-Negro nongeographic central jurisdiction within the Methodist Church. The Wesleyan Methodist Church and the Pilgrim Holiness Church united to form the Wesleyan Church.

The United Church of Christ and the Christian Church (Disciples of Christ) began union negotiations but subordinated them to the Consultation on Church Union, meanwhile forming partnerships between their national boards. Earlier conversations between the Episcopal Church and the Methodist Church were suspended when they joined the Consultation on Church Union.

The Consultation on Church Union was now the forum for exploration between separated denominations of different traditions or confessions. Principles of Church Union were agreed in 1966 and a Plan of Union was submitted to the churches in 1970. The plan called for merging the nine denominations into one church body. However, studies in the churches revealed that this form of church union was unacceptable to all nine bodies. Having served as an advisor at meetings of the consultation, the director understood the disappointment of those involved in the negotiations. In retrospect this outcome appears less surprising because of the wide range of traditions involved and the American context. Restoring visible unity is a process by which the people of each uniting body share the best gifts they have received in their tradition and are willing to take the like from the others. In its next phase the consultation would seek a process adequate to the challenge as well as explore alternative forms or models of visible unity.

In this period another type of consultation on church union proliferated. It was not new. Since 1961 the U.S.A. National Committee of the Lutheran World Federation and the North American Area of the World Alliance of Reformed Churches had been meeting for theological discussion of their historic differences and had already reached agreement on the doctrine of the Lord's Supper. The Anglican-Orthodox Theological Consultation in the United States began their meetings in 1962. The Roman Catholic Church pursued this kind of dialogue nationally and internationally after Vatican II. In the United States, the Bishops' Committee began dialogues with the Lutheran, Episcopal, and Reformed churches in 1965 and the Methodist, Orthodox, American Baptist, and Disciples churches in 1966. Lutheran-Orthodox, Orthodox-Methodist, Reformed-Orthodox, Episcopal-Lutheran, and Catholic–Southern Baptist dialogues were also initiated. Alongside the Consultation on Church Union, these varied bilateral dialogues helped to clarify the churches' understandings of the ecumenical problematic and its contemporary challenges.

Local Ecumenism

A consensus was forming that in principle the search for unity is the responsibility of all members of the body of Christ. Formal bilateral dialogues and church union negotiations would be fruitless if unaccompanied by appropriate dialogue, response, and action by the people of God. The 1961 assembly of the World Council at New Delhi had built this into its classic definition of the ecumenical goal when it used the phrase "all in each place." How could this be implemented? Richard N. Johnson was seconded by the Christian Church (Disciples of Christ) as associate director of Faith and Order with particular responsibility for local ecumenism, to clarify the most suitable and expeditious means.[27]

Councils of churches were already planning regional and state Faith and Order conferences in which nonmember churches increasingly participated. These were held in the Pacific Northwest (1965 and 1967), Pacific Southwest (1965 and 1967), New England (1967), Colorado-New Mexico (1968), and Minnesota, Pennsylvania, Indiana, Ohio, Texas, Virginia, Missouri, and Kentucky. Building on these experiences, Johnson prepared a Handbook for Faith and Order in councils of churches.

Denominations took steps to connect national ecumenical officers and committees with new officers and committees in regional jurisdictions. On the initiative of the Bishops' Committee, a national workshop for Roman Catholic diocesan ecumenical officers began in 1964. Episcopal diocesan ecumenical officers began to meet in 1966. Denominations with different polities began to work on similar lines. In 1969 the Roman Catholic National Association of Diocesan Ecumenical Officers invited Episcopal and other denominational ecumenical officers to join them for a National Workshop on Christian Unity, which provided for both common and denominational meetings. The workshop soon became the most important place for annual national exchange, linking local and national ecumenical officers within and between denominations and providing ecumenical information, education, and inspiration. National ecumenical officers had their own regular meetings and were, in fact, legally responsible for the National Workshop. Faith and Order related closely to these gatherings.

Local and regional initiatives and experiments appeared. Some thrived; others disappeared. One area of special concern was seminary training. In conjunction with the Oberlin conference a North Ameri-

27. "Local Ecumenism," *Faith and Order Trends* 5, no. 3 (June 1965): 1-8.

can Association of Professors Teaching Ecumenics was formed. Later it formed a partnership with the American Association of Theological Schools. Renamed the North American Academy of Ecumenists in 1967, the organization was broadened to include professors of ecumenism and professional ecumenists from all traditions. Faith and Order related to the academy.

The National Council departments of Ministry and Faith and Order jointly sponsored a consultation on Ecumenical Planning for Clergy Training in 1967, co-chaired by Franklin Clark Fry and James I. McCord. It was to identify the opportunities and issues where ecumenical thinking and planning should be initiated. Meanwhile the seminaries were reaching out to each other to form associations or consortia such as the Graduate Theological Union in Berkeley, California, and the Boston Theological Institute. They opened the way to theological education in a setting of interconfessional dialogue so as to better equip ministers and priests with the education needed in a pluralistic society. The older Interseminary Movement continued its seminarian exchanges and a liaison with Faith and Order until its national organization was dissolved along with that of the National Student Christian Federation in 1969, the result of anti-institutional sentiment.

It may be noted that as early as 1955 the National Council had a special committee to guide and supervise studies of ecumenical education. When Faith and Order arrived in 1959 it joined this work.

Other Religions and Nonbelievers

The issue of dialogue with other religions as well as nonreligious stances came to greater prominence in the 1960s. It figured in proposals for future studies at the Montreal Conference on Faith and Order, and the commission meeting at Aarhus in 1964 initiated studies on creation and the work of the triune God in nature and history and in the church. The conviction took hold that if the churches were to grow into unity they had increasingly to apply themselves to central questions before which they all stand in the same perplexity. The questions included other religious and secular faiths.

In 1967 the general assembly of the National Council directed Faith and Order to pursue, in cooperation with others, the study of theological questions as a guide to dialogue with other religions and with nonbelievers. The Faith and Order committee began by studying dialogue between biblical and scientific worldviews and ways to prepare for dialogue with other religions.

The first national meeting of Christians and Jews to deal with other than practical issues took place in 1967, sponsored by the National Council, the Bishops' Committee on Ecumenical (and now) Interreligious Affairs, and the Synagogue Council of America. The theme was The Role of Conscience and its purpose was to analyze the effectiveness of religious organizations in social action by exploring the process through which conscience comes into being.

The prominence of the Jewish community in the United States and the recent occurrence of the Holocaust made it the most significant religion for the churches. In 1969 a study titled Israel: People, Land, State brought together twenty-five scholars and staff of the National Council and the Secretariat for Catholic-Jewish Relations of the National Conference of Catholic Bishops. The study sought to clarify the significance of the theology of the land in the Jewish tradition.

Uppsala: Unity and Ethics

The fourth assembly of the World Council met in Sweden at Uppsala in 1968, with the Orthodox now the largest delegation. Foremost in delegates' minds were the crises in the world. The recently slain Martin Luther King Jr. was to have preached at the opening worship. The assembly declared the evil of racism to be "a blatant denial of the Christian faith." Despair about the pace of development in poor nations produced a call to the churches to work for the vindication of the rights of the poor and oppressed, and for economic justice and peace in the world.

While the assembly understood the connection between unity and ethics in global mission, it did not assume that unity in service of the world could by itself lead to unity of the churches. Action was taken to complete the New Delhi statement:

So to the emphasis on "all in each place" (at New Delhi) we would now add a fresh understanding of the unity of all Christians in all places. This calls the churches in all places to realize that they belong together and are called to act together. In a time when human interdependence is so evident, it is the more imperative to make visible the bonds which unite Christians in universal fellowship. . . .

Some real experience of universality is provided by establishing regional and international confessional fellowships. But such experiences of universality are inevitably partial. The ecumenical movement helps to enlarge this experience of universality, and its regional councils and its World Council may be regarded as a transitional opportunity for eventually actualizing a truly universal, ecumenical, conciliar form of common life and witness. The members of the World Council of Churches, committed to each other, should work for the time when a genuinely universal council may once more speak for all Christians, and lead the way into the future.[28]

This was notable as the first formal proposal of a goal for all levels of the ecumenical movement. State and local councils were virtually everywhere in the United States. The proposal of a "genuinely universal council" had resonance.

Three Relationships

In the 1960s people felt they were living in the midst of an ecumenical miracle. It did not produce unions between separated denominations of *different* traditions, but it created a new climate of friendship among the people of the churches and stimulated a new vision of the unity of humankind. People of this generation were the first to glimpse the challenge of shaping the *whole* church for mission. Much needed

28. Norman Goodall, ed., *The Uppsala Report* (Geneva: World Council of Churches, 1968), p. 17.

to be done if contemporary insights into the nature, form, and responsibility of the church were to replace old models. The possibility of a second North American Faith and Order Conference was discussed.

Relationships with the Orthodox Church of the east (now in the west) were the first of three areas where better information was needed before a North American conference. A project of interviews with bishops and theologians of the churches of Constantinople and Greece was begun in 1969 by Arthur Dore of the Office of Inter-Church Relations of the Greek Orthodox Archdiocese of North and South America and by the director of Faith and Order.[29] The positions of these churches were influential within orthodoxy.

Since the 1920 encyclical on the ecumenical movement from the Ecumenical Patriarch, the Orthodox emphasis had been on practical problems and on theological dialogues with Anglican and Protestant churches in the west. After Vatican II an Orthodox-Catholic "dialogue of love" began, but the "dialogue of truth" lay in the future. Substantial agreement had been reached by official dialogues between the Orthodox and the Oriental Orthodox churches (non-Chalcedonian) and the Old Catholic Church. In the United States, Orthodox had conversations with Catholics, Anglicans, and Protestants, but these did not have the authority of the international Pan-Orthodox Conference. The interviews in Istanbul and Greece clarified the Orthodox principle of "one city one bishop," but it was recognized that practical adjustments are sometimes needed. It was wrong to identify the bishop with a "rite" and allow parallel jurisdictions as practiced by the Roman Catholic Church.

Neither theological dialogue nor joint action should be so stressed as to minimize the other. In the interview with Ecumenical Patriarch Athenagoras it was said, "The truth is Jesus Christ, the way, the truth, and life. Christ will bring unity as we try to make Christ. It is the living of the gospel . . . love." This reminded us of a remark by Nikos Nissiotis that it is not dogma or jealousies that caused division, but the lack of *koinonia* between the local churches.

29. "Report of Greek Orthodoxy and the Ecumenical Movement," unpublished Faith and Order paper (1969).

The Orthodox Church lived everywhere under severe difficulties. It lacked the freedom from the state that churches in the west enjoyed, so it could not be a growing Orthodoxy and make its full contribution in the ecumenical movement. In America alone the Orthodox lived in substantial numbers with religious freedom alongside Protestants, Anglicans, and Catholics. Here the theological problems all churches faced could give the dialogue a contemporary reference, whereas in the east the churches tended to take up the dialogue where it had left off many centuries ago. In America a high priority should be given to doctrinal and ecclesiological studies of east and west. It was here that the Orthodox should, with the assistance of Protestant and Catholic theologians, take up the task until the whole of Orthodoxy is ready.

The growth of evangelical bodies was the second area where fuller information was needed. In 1969 the first U.S. Congress on Evangelism had 4,700 delegates from almost one hundred denominations, some of them member churches of the National Council. The call to apply Christianity to social problems was in almost every address.[30] A paper from Leighton Ford of the Billy Graham Association declared, "We cannot be worthy of our high calling if we try to keep God in some private, undisturbed corner of our lives and ignore the driving winds of change. . . . We know that sin infects every man and every institution. So we need a holy discontent with the status quo." He held "no brief for James Forman's 'Black Manifesto.' Yet if our reaction is simply to lash back at Forman and if we do not seek to heal the gaping, aching, rubbed-raw wounds of racial strife, then we shall deserve 'the fire next time.' . . . [T]he right of men to freedom, dignity, and respect comes directly from the Bible. . . . We know there are 'Bible belts' where the Gospel is preached and people are converted but where there are built-in structures and attitudes of prejudice that change very slowly. That does not mean that people are not converted, but it does mean that the Holy Spirit has a great deal of work to do in our hearts and minds after conversion."

Ford observed that "revolutionary action in evangelism . . . will

30. Leighton Ford quoted in "Evangelicals Called to Social Involvement," *Unity Trends* 2, no. 24 (December 1969).

mean acting with other Christians from other churches. Our task is to confront everyone with the Gospel, and no one church can accomplish that job." *Christianity Today* editorialized: "Perhaps no evangelical conclave in this century has responded more positively to the call for Christians to help right wrongs in the social order. Those who listened carefully realized that the call to social involvement was put on a personal basis. Thus there was avoided what so many evangelicals believe to be a major error of the ecumenical movement, that of making the institutional church the agent of social revolution as though that were the mission of the Church." It would not escape our attention that both the congress and the National Faith and Order colloquium on Salvation and Life signaled some convergence, though by no means an identity of positions, and that dialogue about the purpose of the church was an imperative.

The third relationship requiring attention was the Roman Catholic Church. After Vatican II the question of Catholic membership in the National Council as the most prominent national ecumenical body inevitably arose. In 1969 a Joint Study Committee began to work through the practical, pastoral, and theological problems in the event of an application for membership. Meanwhile, Bernard F. Law succeeded William W. Baum in 1967 as executive director of the Bishops' Committee and was in turn succeeded by John F. Hotchkin in 1971.

The study committee dealt with many issues: overcoming Christian divisions, critiques of institutional ecumenism, mutual recognition of member churches, the ecclesiastical status and "basis" of the council, common policies and programs, relations with other constituencies, the nature of the national Roman Catholic Church, staff, representation, and finance. Its report concluded that "in substance, nearly every argument in favor of the continuation of the NCC (or a comparable successor) is also an argument for Roman Catholic membership." A decision whether the arguments were sufficiently weighty to bring about an application for membership naturally had to be made by church leadership.

The report appeared in 1972.[31] Near the end of the study process it

31. *Report on Possible Roman Catholic Membership in the National Council of*

seemed to some that an application was unlikely. The report itself suggested two deterrents. One was that a few policy statements or programs of the council might not be welcome (abortion, population control, divorce, and public aid to church-related schools are cited). The church could, like other member churches, issue a minority report or accumulate votes to stop approval. Another problem was that a large financial commitment would be expected from what would be the largest member church by far.

Five years later Archbishop Joseph L. Bernardin of Chicago, then president of the National Conference of Catholic Bishops, told the council's general board that there was more willingness to cooperate at the top leadership level than among staffs of the U.S. Catholic Conference and the National Council. On the question of membership in the council he said "the people are not ready for this yet," but a good deal of progress had been made regarding membership in regional and local councils of churches.

The possibility of a wider national ecumenical body faded, even though the Roman Catholic Church became a full member of many national councils in Africa, Asia, and Europe. In the United States it may have been a mistake to invite a very large church into membership rather than to propose negotiating a successor body. As financial resources dwindled in the following years, the council went through a series of restructures, though its basic nature did not change. Some were unwilling to relinquish the idea of a wider and deeper ecumenical engagement and thought that Faith and Order might lead the way.

The Faith and Order secretariat grew in 1968 with the appointment of Sister Ann Patrick Ware, S.L., as assistant director, believed to be the first theologian of her gender to serve on any Faith and Order staff. Richard W. Rousseau, S.J., was appointed an assistant director in 1969 and Edward Delaney, S.A., was named executive assistant. The three were seconded from their religious orders with the encouragement of the Bishops' Commission. Associate director Richard N. Johnson left

---

Churches by the Study Committee on the Relationship of the National Council of Churches and the Roman Catholic Church in the United States of America (Washington, DC: United States Catholic Conference, 1972).

the staff in 1970. David Bowman, S.J., left to became special assistant to the general secretary and an assistant director of the National Council Commission on Regional and Local Ecumenism. The Division of Christian Unity was deactivated in 1970 because of finances, and the Commission on Faith and Order was again related directly to the general board. All council bodies were seeking the voices of more women and minorities in their work.

A Second North American Faith and Order Conference

The Commission on Faith and Order judged in 1969 that the time had come for a second North American Conference on Faith and Order as an instrument of ecumenical appraisal and involvement. The director's report to the general board that year spoke about the current state of Christian unity in the United States.[32] James I. McCord proposed and the board voted in favor of a North American conference in the early 1970s, open to member and nonmember Christian bodies, with appropriate advice from other units of the council in developing the program, and with the collaboration of councils of churches and the participation of churches in other nations of North America (Canada, Mexico, and the Caribbean to be contacted). McCord's address to the board was heard in the context of the "crisis in the nation," the struggle for civil rights and peace:

> Our old images are outdated, and not even the model of the Church of South India can modernize them. There is much work to be done within the North American context, if contemporary insights into the new shape and tasks for the Church at home and abroad are to replace obsolete models. The best theological resources of the churches must be challenged to this task. There is a desperate need for an ecclesiology for the future, a fresh and imperious image of the shape and paths of the Church tomorrow.

32. "Crisis and Promise in the Ecumenical Movement," *Unity Trends* 2, no. 14 (June 1969): 1-12; and 2, no. 15 (June 1969): 5-8.

Moreover, we have caught a new vision of common witness and service to mankind. With this vision there has come a crisis in authority, a deep restlessness in the Church, and a questioning of almost every aspect of religious faith and practice. There is a demand for change in the way authority is exercised, a clamor for broader participation in decision making at all levels of the Church.[33]

The commission and secretariat set to work. Preparatory studies were expected to play a part in giving new impetus, purposefulness, and expectancy to the process that seemed to be shaping the ecumenical movement. The promise was that an effective participation was possible from nearly all parts of Christianity in North America. Convergence concerning faith seemed further advanced than most would have expected, and on matters of order there was progress. A delegated conference was needed to test and to present this fresh image and potency of unity to the people of the churches and people of the nations. Some provision would be made for voicing the experience of Christians in Central and South America.

The assemblies of both the Canadian Council of Churches and the National Council of Churches, meeting in their respective nations in 1969, supported the conference. A date was set for 1972. Early in 1971 Bishop Joseph L. Bernardin, then general secretary of the National Conference of Catholic Bishops, told the general board that the bishops had decided to participate in the conference as members of the Commission on Faith and Order.

Preparations were halted in 1971 when the commission received a joint memorandum from the director and from its new chairman, Robert J. Marshall, president of the Lutheran Church in America, stating that its executive committee had no choice but to give priority attention to financing. The council administration had said that an accumulated deficit must be repaid. The director would be leaving the staff. Ware and Rousseau would continue with stipends far below nor-

---

33. James I. McCord, "North American Ecumenical Conference," *Unity Trends* 2, no. 15 (June 1969): 2-4.

mal salary levels. The commission could not continue to plan for the North American conference.

Designated support from the churches for Faith and Order had remained steady through the national economic recession in the late 1960s. A special appeal from Marshall brought increased contributions from some churches, but inflation in the economy offset them. The commission requested help from council general funds, but none were available. Later Marshall resigned as chairman of the Faith and Order Commission.

General secretary R. H. Edwin Espy told the general board that the executive director's "leadership in his twelve years in the Council has given to Faith and Order a major place in the work of the Council which was unthinkable and even actively opposed by many at the time the Council was organized." Continuing financial shortfalls in the 1970s mandated staff reductions across the council.

How may we evaluate the loss of a more representative conference of North American Christians to respond to challenges to the churches and the ecumenical movement? An institutional survival mode began to prevail in church and council circles. The council responded to financial challenges by repeated restructuring — focusing on goals, strategies, and organizational design. Much energy and money was spent on these efforts. The council continued but did not become a wider center of communication *(koinonia)* between U.S. churches. To its credit, the council sustained Faith and Order in its more modest structure. It fell to Faith and Order to develop and maintain communication with a wider circle of churches.

A national conference was lost in the conflict between two desirable ends: new models for the shape and tasks of the church in North America, and conserving or maintaining the council as an institution supporting the ecumenical movement. The Consultation on Church Union would continue to address the need for new models, but it directly concerned only nine churches. The galvanizing contribution of a North American conference for all the churches at a critical point for unity and mission was not to be.

Louvain: Unity and Human Community

The director still had time to be an adviser at the World Council Commission on Faith and Order at Louvain in 1971. It met under the comprehensive theme The Unity of the Church — the Unity of Humankind. Subthemes were (1) the struggle for justice and society, (2) the encounter with other living faiths, (3) the struggle against racism, (4) the role of the handicapped in society, and (5) differences of cultures. Differences surfaced between those who resisted linking the search for unity with the struggle for human community and those who insisted that unity and mission had to be a voice of liberation and reconciliation. Louvain set in motion a study to address these differences. Section discussions focused on the authority of the Bible, giving account of the hope that is in us, catholicity and apostolicity, worship today, baptism — confirmation — eucharist, ordained ministry, the council of Chalcedon, common witness and proselytism, conciliarity, and church union negotiations and bilateral conversations.

Back in the United States a 1971 presentation to the general board focused on Faith and Order's position and funding in the National Council. Robert T. Handy of the American Baptist Church, now chair of the commission, presented the rationale from a historical perspective. Other presentations were The Black Experience and Faith and Order by William T. Kennedy of Yale Divinity School; Expectations of Faith and Order by Robert Moss, president of the United Church of Christ; A Roman Catholic Statement; Local and Regional Ecumenical Needs for Faith and Order by James M. Webb of the Connecticut Council of Churches; and A Short History of the Relation of Faith and Order within the National Council by the director. Daniel Day Williams of Union Theological Seminary reflected on Louvain:

> We are witnessing an increasing polarization between those who see the church through its tradition and cherish above all its continuity and those who seek radical reconstruction of church life and ministry to serve the new world. This polarization is potentially creative, provided it does not split Christians into opposing camps who cannot understand one another. To

51

maintain communication between those holding different perspectives is in considerable part a theological problem. It requires informed and creative approaches to the meaning of faith, ministry and church, and to saying what the Christian Gospel is in relation to contemporary thought.[34]

34. Unpublished document of the National Council general board.

CHAPTER II

Many Voices

When the euphoria produced by the ecumenical "miracle" of the 1960s began to wane, some began to wonder whether the movement was running out of steam or like a clock winding down. Others thought it was having "growing pains," the result of changed relationships and wider participation on all levels. It is true that significant movements pass through different stages, changing in ways consistent with their purpose and dynamic.

Trends in society and in the churches demanded attention. Some examples were a dislike of bigness and corporatism, an emphasis on localism-regionalism, suspicion of authority, demands for rights of minorities, changing sexual mores, and a positive evaluation of diversity coupled with emphasis on cultural and ethnic heritages. Increasing numbers of Muslims and adherents of other faiths were entering the United States. New spiritual movements and cults were proliferating. Theologians focused on experiences of human suffering, injustice, and oppression, leading to criticisms of Christian tradition and discovery of new resources within it. Feminist and other liberation theologians understood Christian praxis, the life of discipleship, to set both foundations and goals for theology.

Changes in the balance of Christian influence also occurred. Membership of so-called "mainline" churches declined while conservative Evangelical, Pentecostal, and other bodies not members of the National Council flourished. The council was more on the margins, with less access to the media. Changes in this balance became a central reality for Faith and Order, as Jeffrey Gros, F.S.C., noted later:

> For the U.S. churches not involved in bilateral dialogues, church union negotiations, and not selected for service on the World Council Commission, Faith and Order NCCC becomes the unique area available to them for discussion of the church dividing/church uniting issues. The forty member churches (of the commission), including the two largest communities — Southern Baptist and Roman Catholic — find here their only access to many ecumenical partners, since their paths cross neither at NCCC General Board, NAE Theology Commission meetings, nor at other vehicles for ecclesiological reconciliation. For some of the Peace, Pentecostal, African-American, Holiness and smaller churches, this working group is the only area for theological, ecumenical conversation, and the only access to a broad range of ecumenical partners.[1]

Jorge Lara-Braud of the Presbyterian Church became the second director of Faith and Order late in 1972, and Richard Rousseau left the secretariat. The first meeting of the commission in 1973 reflected a refocusing of Faith and Order in the restructured council, which, as Handy noted, was premised on the conviction that there are "theological and unitive dimensions" in all the council does. The danger of turning Faith and Order into the theological department of the council was avoided, and a wider range of topics would be embraced.

A Statement to Our Fellow Christians emerged in 1973 from the study Israel: People, Land, State, which, as noted above, began in 1969 jointly sponsored by Faith and Order and the secretariat for Catholic-Jewish Relations of the National Conference of Catholic Bishops. It was distributed to Jewish and Christian groups, accompanied by questions for study and response.[2] The National Council opened an office

1. Jeffrey Gros, F.S.C., "The Vision of Christian Unity: Some Aspects of Faith and Order in the Context of United States Culture," *Mid-Stream* 30, no. 1 (January 1999): 1.
2. "A Statement to Our Fellow Christians," *Ecumenical Trends* 2, no. 5 (August 1973): 5-12.

on Christian-Jewish relations staffed by William L. Weiler that year. And the biannual National Workshop on Catholic-Jewish Relations was launched. At its second meeting it was renamed Christian-Jewish Relations and was sponsored jointly by the secretariat for Catholic-Jewish relations and the National Council office on Christian-Jewish relations. This arrangement would continue until the late 1990s, when a council for centers on Christian-Jewish relations became the central vehicle for communication between the two faiths.

Regional Faith and Order consultations took place at Atlanta in 1973 and 1974, producing a report titled Points at Issue Between Black and White Theologies.[3] Three other regional clusters discussed Pioneering a Hunger-Free World: Beyond the Survival Strategy of Lifeboats and Battlefields, Community of Women and Men in the Church (but see below), and The Tension Between Confessional Positions and Ecumenical Commitments, but produced no reports. Such topics as these were also discussed in the churches, but it was difficult to reach consensus and few publications emerged from the Faith and Order commission at this time.

The National Council established a Christian-Muslim task force in 1976. It was administratively related to Faith and Order and staffed by Byron Haines and Marston Speight. The task force relocated to Hartford Seminary in the 1980s.

In response to numerous requests a statement was prepared titled A Critique of the Theology of the Unification Church as Set Forth in "Divine Principle."[4] After reviewing the main teachings in its official text, the statement concluded that the Unification Church is not a Christian church and its claims to Christian identity could not be recognized.

In view of the current controversies in the churches, the commission issued A Call to Responsible Ecumenical Debate on Controversial Issues: Abortion and Homosexuality in 1979.[5] It describes the role of

3. Summary of "Points at Issue Between Black and White Theologies," *Ecumenical Trends* 4, no. 3 (March 1975): 43-45.

4. Summary of "A Critique of the Theology of the Unification Church as Set Forth in 'Divine Principle,'" *Ecumenical Trends* 6, no. 8 (September 1977): 125-26.

5. "A Call to Responsible Ecumenical Dialogue on Controversial Issues: Abortion and Homosexuality," *Ecumenical Trends* 8, no. 3 (March 1979): 45-48. Reprinted in *Ecu-*

sustaining faith in communities dealing with theological and ethical conflicts and suggests topics for study.

Coming Together in the Spirit, a volume authored by Frederick Borsch, was based on a Faith and Order study titled Spirituality for Ecumenism.[6] It describes the heritage Christians retain despite their divisions and suggests how a fuller sharing in the common spiritual treasure can be approached in this situation.

Community of Women and Men

Initiated by the World Council Faith and Order commission meeting at Accra in 1974, a study of The Community of Women and Men in the Church took up such issues as the language, symbols, and imagery in scripture and in the churches as they influence men-women relationships and the ordination of women. Conducted in consultation with the World Council unit on Women in Church and Society, it was staffed from 1978 by Constance F. Parvey. Study groups throughout the world used an experience-based method of theological reflection.

Contributions from the American groups were collated for a United States Section Report by Kathryn Johnson Lieurance. William Jerry Boney of the Presbyterian Church, appointed third director to succeed Lara-Braud in 1980, took great interest in the study but died suddenly in 1981. Jeffrey Gros, F.S.C., of the Roman Catholic Church, who succeeded Ann Patrick Ware as associate in 1981, was named fourth director in 1982. Reflections from a group of theologians and pastors on the United States Section Report were summarized by Madeleine Boucher.[7] This material, along with reports from other parts of the world, was studied by a consultation at Sheffield, England, in 1981. This study process made plain that there would be no unity without

---

menical Documents IV: Building Unity, ed Joseph A. Burgess and Jeffrey Gros, F.S.C. (New York: Paulist Press, 1989), pp. 453-57.

6. Frederick Borsch, *Coming Together in the Spirit* (Cincinnati: Forward Movement Publications and Nashville: Upper Room, 1980).

7. Madeleine Boucher, "Authority in Community," *Mid-Stream* 21, no. 3 (July 1982): 402-17.

making visible the full and equal representation of all peoples at all
levels of the church's life. The study helped to increase the participation of women in meetings of the World Council, including women
theologians in Faith and Order. The inclusion of women in ordination
would continue to be a subject of controversy.

Nairobi: Unity and Conciliar Fellowship

At the fifth assembly of the World Council at Nairobi in 1975, Faith
and Order topics included the community of women and men, the
coming statement on Baptism, Eucharist and Ministry, and the vision
of conciliar fellowship. The Uppsala assembly in 1968 had said that the
churches should "work for a time when a genuinely ecumenical council may once more speak for all Christians and lead the way into the
future." The Faith and Order Commission took this up at Louvain in
1971 and held a consultation in 1973 at Salamanca on Concepts of
Unity and Models of Union. The Nairobi assembly reaffirmed the
New Delhi statement on "all in each place," combined it with the
Uppsala dimension of unity as "catholicity," and adopted the description of conciliar fellowship formulated at Salamanca:

> The one Church is to be envisioned as a conciliar fellowship of
> local churches which are themselves truly united. In this
> conciliar fellowship, each local church possesses, in communion
> with the others, the fullness of catholicity, witnesses to the same
> apostolic faith, and therefore recognizes the others as belonging
> to the same Church of Christ and guided by the same Spirit.
> They are one in their common commitment to confess the gospel of Christ by proclamation and service to the world. To this
> end, each church aims at maintaining sustained and sustaining
> relationships with her sister churches, expressed in conciliar
> gatherings whenever required for the fulfillment of their common calling.
>
> The term is intended to describe an aspect of the life of the
> one undivided Church *at all levels*. In the first place, it expresses

the unity of church separated by distance, culture, and time, a unity which is publicly manifested when the representatives of these local churches gather together for a common meeting. It also refers to a quality of life within each local church; it underlies the fact that true unity is not monolithic, does not override the special gifts given to each member and to each local church, but rather cherishes and protects them.[8]

The National Council of Faith and Order set to work reflecting on the Nairobi statement in the U.S. context. Its group on Conciliar Fellowship, coordinated from 1977 to 1981 by William A. Norgren, emphasized reconciliation among races, sexes, and classes as a central aspect of the goal of unity. Its report consists of three sections: (1) Conciliar Fellowship and a Universal Council of the Church: Their Meaning and Necessity; (2) A Universal Council of the Church: Creating the Conditions through Conciliar Fellowship; and (3) The American Way of Life, Conciliar Fellowship, and a Universal Council. The report was critiqued in the commission and discussed in seminars at a National Council "Ecumenical Event" held at Cleveland in 1981 to celebrate the council's thirtieth anniversary. The report was published with a summary of the discussions and transmitted to the World Council.[9]

Fellowships, Communities, and Covenants

Whether or not they were stimulated by the vision of conciliar fellowship, church-to-church relationships were multiplying. The Consultation on Church Union sought to reorient its work after the participating churches found the first Plan of Union unacceptable. In 1974 it asked member churches officially to recognize each other's baptized members. All did so. Two projects began, aimed at developing a new

8. David M. Paton, ed., *Breaking Barriers, Nairobi, 1975* (London: SPCK, 1976), p. 60.

9. "Conciliar Fellowship," *Mid-Stream* 21, no. 2 (April 1982): 243-72. Reprinted in Burgess and Gros, eds., *Ecumenical Documents IV*, pp. 458-83.

model of church union. One was Interim Eucharistic Fellowships, which were occasional, though regular, gatherings at the eucharist of members of congregations who would not ordinarily celebrate together. It was hoped that shared mission would emerge from these. The other was Generating Communities, gatherings of representatives from several congregations to design their own structures for shared worship and mission "as they live and work toward union." Task forces were organized on institutional racism, women, worship, structures for mission, and the disabled. Revision of the first Plan of Union was assigned to a theological commission, which sent the text In Quest of a Church of Christ Uniting: An Emerging Theological Consensus to the churches in 1976 for study and response. A further chapter on the ministry was dispatched in 1979. A commission on governance was to receive information from all of the above.

Interparish covenants were springing up. These were written agreements between two congregations of different traditions committing themselves to prayer for each other at Sunday worship, worship together on special occasions, dialogue, and joint work on mission tasks. Covenants were formally ratified at a service of worship. Most were Episcopal-Catholic, Lutheran-Episcopal, or Lutheran-Catholic, but Presbyterian, Methodist, United, Disciples, and Orthodox congregations were involved too. Such covenants were a more enduring, though not necessarily permanent, form of interparish relationship. Covenanted congregations responded to the reports from the bilateral dialogues conducted by their communions. Some became three-way relationships. Some shared buildings and church programs (with or without common worship) for reasons of missionary strategy while they maintained their denominational identities.

Such arrangements — fellowships, communities, and covenants — were understood as expressions of existing unity; sometimes as interim forms of conciliar fellowship. Some covenants were initiated between dioceses and synods, campus ministries, and religious orders. Denominations often invited representatives of other denominations to participate in national or regional synods and conventions, with or without voice or vote.

National Council Affairs

Restructuring reached a further stage with the creation of a study panel on Ecumenical Commitment and National Council of Churches Purposes, led by Paul A. Crow of the Christian Church (Disciples of Christ) and Faith and Order chairwoman Jeanne Audrey Powers of the United Methodist Church. The panel produced a new preamble to the constitution, defining the council as "a community of communions" in place of "a cooperative agency of the churches." An ecclesiological word, *koinonia,* defined the nature of the council instead of an organizational word, *agency.* After this and other changes in 1981, the renamed governing board of the council continued to hear presentations on issues of visible unity, but focused mainly on urgent issues of the day and governance.

Based on work done by Faith and Order and the North American Academy of Ecumenists, the governing board adopted a resolution in 1981 urging the World Council and the Vatican to prepare an ecumenical celebration for the year 2000. The proposal called for a celebration of ecumenical progress to date in the context of conciliar fellowship. It was not implemented.[10]

A governing board panel studying questions of bioethics invited Faith and Order to provide theological reflections that would undergird its work on a public policy statement. Recommendations from the commission, now with William G. Rusch as chairman, were summarized in 1982 by J. Robert Nelson, accompanied by a statement from a group of women in the commission.

Formation of the Metropolitan Community Church, with a mainly gay and lesbian membership, led eventually to an application for membership in the National Council. The governing board requested Faith and Order, not to make a recommendation on its eligibility (the responsibility of another committee), but to clarify issues of ecclesiology and ecumenical fellowship in the life of the council. The Faith and Order report in 1983 was titled The Church, the Churches

---

10. Lewis S. Mudge, "Toward a Truly Ecumenical Council," *Mid-Stream* 26, no. 4 (October 1987): 494-505.

and the Metropolitan Church. It takes the form of a dialogue between representatives of member churches and the Metropolitan Church.[11]

Bilateral and Multilateral Dialogues

Dialogues organized by councils of churches comprising many traditions or confessions (multilateral) were characteristic of the ecumenical movement before the 1960s. In the years following, dialogues organized by Christian world communions between two traditions or confessions (bilateral) began to multiply. It became apparent that the two types of dialogue had different characteristics and tasks that needed to be interrelated. World Council Faith and Order, which had long arranged periodic consultations for united and uniting churches, initiated a forum in 1978 for bilateral dialogues. In this way the trends and results of the numerous bilaterals could be compared multilaterally.

National Council Faith and Order formed a study group on bilateral conversations coordinated by Daniel F. Martensen in 1981. It looked at the topics taken up in reports of both bilateral and multilateral dialogues and the assumptions that seemed implicit. Next, it asked about the "reception" of dialogue results, understood as their assimilation and integration into the theology, educational systems, and life of the local churches. Tensions between those who emphasized the importance of one or the other type of dialogue were addressed.

In view of continuing difficulties of reaching consensus in the commission, Faith and Order began to hold consultations and conferences intended to unearth and publish important information. One of these, titled Bilateral and Multilateral Dialogues in the One Ecumenical Movement, was sponsored jointly with the Washington Institute of

11. Jeffrey Gros, ed., "The Church, the Churches and the Metropolitan Church," *Mid-Stream* 22, nos. 3 and 4 (July/October 1983): 453-67. Narrative in *The Ecumenical Review* 36, no. 1 (January 1984): 71-81. A reprint is retitled "Faith and Order Commission Report on the Application for Membership in the NCCC of the Universal Fellowship of Metropolitan Community Churches," in *Growing Consensus I: Church Dialogues in the United States, 1962-1991*, ed. Joseph A. Burgess and Jeffrey Gros, F.S.C. (New York: Paulist Press, 1995), pp. 614-28.

Ecumenics in 1984. It reported thirty-four findings on (1) aspects of conversion in ecumenical dialogue, (2) the nature of the unity we seek, and (3) the faith and order of the church and the future of ecumenical dialogue. This report and the papers prepared by the study group were published in 1986 and 1989.[12]

It is interesting to note that the Consultation on Church Union is unique in exhibiting characteristics of both a multilateral and a bilateral dialogue. Multilaterally it involved nine churches representing Episcopal, Disciples, Methodist, and Reformed traditions, though without the usual wider range of traditions found in multilateral dialogues. Bilaterally it involved one-on-one dialogues between certain of these traditions as well as a significant dialogue between three African American churches and six predominantly white churches.

After completing the local projects and theological work already described, in 1984 the consultation adopted The COCU Consensus: In Quest of a Church Uniting. The participating churches were asked to recognize in it "an expression, in the matters with which it deals, of the apostolic faith, order, worship and witness of the church," "an anticipation of the Church Uniting which the participating bodies, by the power of the Holy Spirit, wish to become," and "a sufficient theological basis for the covenanting acts and uniting process proposed at this time by the Consultation." In 1988 the consultation adopted Churches in Covenant Communion: The Church of Christ Uniting, which offered proposals for covenanting and inaugural liturgies. According to this plan the participating churches would become one in faith, sacraments, ministry, and mission, but existing polities and practices would be left unchanged. The churches were asked to approve the document as the "definitive agreement" for entering into covenant communion.

---

12. Daniel F. Martensen, ed., "The Quest for Christian Consensus: A Study of Bilateral Theological Dialogue in the Ecumenical Movement," *Journal of Ecumenical Studies* 23, no. 3 (Summer 1986): 361-544. A description of the 1984 Washington consultation appears in *Mid-Stream* 24, no. 1 (January 1985). John Ford, ed., "A Report on the Bilateral and Multilateral Dialogues in the One Ecumenical Movement," *Mid-Stream* 28, no. 1 (January 1989): 115-36. Reprinted as "A Report of the Bilateral Study Group of the Faith and Order Commission of the National Council of Churches," in Burgess and Gros, eds., *Growing Consensus I*, pp. 629-48.

Meanwhile two major unions between churches of the same tradition or confession occurred. The Presbyterian Church (U.S.A.) was formed by the Presbyterian Church U.S. (southern) and the United Presbyterian Church in the United States of America (northern) in 1983. The Evangelical Lutheran Church in America was formed in 1988 by the American Lutheran Church, the Lutheran Church in America, and the Association of Evangelical Lutheran Churches.

Vancouver: Unity and Human Renewal

The sixth World Council assembly, which convened at Vancouver in 1983, reaffirmed the Nairobi statement on conciliar fellowship and added the need for (1) a common understanding of the apostolic faith; (2) the mutual recognition of baptism, eucharist, and ministry; and (3) a search for common ways of decision making. It also confronted a major tension within the ecumenical movement:

> For some, the search for a unity in one faith and one eucharistic fellowship seems, at best secondary, at worst irrelevant to the struggles for peace, justice and human dignity; for others the church's political involvement against the evils of history seems, at best secondary, at worst detrimental to its role in eucharistic community and witness to the gospel.[13]

The assembly declared, "As Christians we want to affirm there can be no such division between unity and human renewal, either in the church or in the agenda of the WCC." Baptism, eucharist, and ministry are "healing and uniting signs of a church living and working for a renewed and reconciled humankind"; and racism, classism, and sexism call for a common struggle, since "no one form of renewal will, by itself, accomplish a renewal of ecclesial community."[14] The assembly

---

13. David Gill, ed., *Gathered for Life* (Geneva: WCC Publications, 1983), p. 49.
14. Excerpts quoted by Paul Crow in *Faith and Order 1985-1989*, ed. Thomas F. Best (Geneva: WCC Publications, 1990), p. 136.

suggested a mutually supportive relationship between unity and human renewal through its call to the member churches to engage in a conciliar process of mutual commitment to justice, peace, and the integrity of creation.

Baptism, Eucharist and Ministry

At Lima, Peru, in 1982, the World Council commission on Faith and Order unanimously approved the text Baptism, Eucharist and Ministry for transmission to the churches. The result of careful scholarship and persistent dialogue over many years, BEM is a "convergence" text that recognizes and formulates a remarkable degree of agreement in three formerly controversial areas. The churches were asked how far they could "recognize in this text the faith of the church through the ages," what consequences they could draw from it for their relations, particularly with other churches that recognize the text as an expression of the apostolic faith, and what guidance they could take from it for their life and witness. BEM would become the most widely publicized, translated, and discussed report in the history of the ecumenical movement.

National Council Faith and Order associated itself in 1983 with the Hyde Park cluster of theological schools for a consultation on the "reception" of BEM, sponsored by the Ecumenical Project of the Jesuit House. Information was collected about the process of reception in the various churches. Persons from charismatic, evangelical, and free churches were drawn into participation. Several publications followed, among them the volume *The Search for Visible Unity*.[15] In 1986, Faith and Order and the Association of Chicago Area Theological Schools jointly sponsored a conference to share the official responses of U.S. churches to BEM.[16] Faith and Order also created a panel at the

15. Jeffrey Gros, "'Baptism, Eucharist and Ministry' and Its Reception in the U.S. Churches," *Journal of Ecumenical Studies* 21, no. 1 (Winter 1984): 1-146. Jeffrey Gros, ed., *The Search for Visible Unity* (New York: Pilgrim Press, 1984).

16. "Baptism, Eucharist and Ministry Conference," *Mid-Stream* 25, no. 3 (July 1986): 322-29. A description of the conference appears in *Ecumenical Trends* 15, no. 10 (November 1986): 169-70. See articles in *American Baptist Quarterly* 7, no. 1 (March

council's governing board on the "Lima Liturgy" based on BEM. The board voted to commend the World Council for BEM and to encourage the reception process in the churches.

Responses to BEM from churches, councils, and theological faculties around the world eventually filled six volumes. World Council Faith and Order was able in 1990 to report on key affirmations and on issues needing further work, namely scripture and tradition, sacraments and sacramentality, and ecclesiology.

The Apostolic Faith Today

At Lima the World Council commission turned its attention to the core of the Christian faith. Building on previous reports such as A Common Account of Hope (1978), which blended classical and contemporary contextual theologies, a study was initiated, titled Towards the Common Expression of the Apostolic Faith Today. The project had three aspects: (1) the common recognition of the apostolic faith as expressed in the ecumenical symbol of the faith, the Nicene Creed; (2) the common explication of this apostolic faith in the contemporary situation of the churches; and (3) a common confession of the apostolic faith today.

In the United States, where there are differences concerning the use of the Nicene Creed and other confessions, this study opened up exceptional opportunities. A Faith and Order study group on The Apostolic Faith as a Basis for Contemporary Ecumenical Witness was coordinated by Glenn Hinson of the Southern Baptist Convention. A topic sure to be considered was the language of the Nicene Creed as it bears on the issue of gender inclusiveness.[17] Individual consultations were arranged with African American, Orthodox, and Pentecostal churches.

1988): 2-77. Report reprinted in Lydia Velko and Jeffrey Gros, F.S.C., eds., *Growing Consensus II: Church Dialogues in the United States 1992-2004* (Washington: U.S. Conference of Catholic Bishops, 2005), pp. 487-95. See also Merle D. Strege, ed., *Baptism and Church: A Believers' Church Vision* (Grand Rapids: Sagamore Books, 1986).

17. Lauree Hersch Meyer, "Language Issues in Studying the Apostolic Faith," *Mid-Stream* 23, no. 4 (October 1984): 412-16. Melanie A. May, "Conversations on Language and Imagery of God," *Union Seminary Quarterly Review* 40, no. 3 (August 1985): 11-20.

The first (1984) of several consultations with African American churches produced the volume *Black Witness to the Apostolic Faith,* which takes up the four creedal marks of the church from the perspectives of racial equity and ethical implications of a consistent ecclesiology.[18] A statement presented to the study group by a consultation in Richmond, Virginia, titled Toward a Common Expression of Faith: A Black North American Perspective is included in this volume and was printed in several journals.[19]

Protestant and Episcopal theologians met (1985) to respond to reports from three earlier dialogues in Europe and the Middle East on Christology: Orthodox–Oriental Orthodox, Catholic–Oriental Orthodox, and Catholic-Assyrian. The results are in the volume *Christ in East and West.*[20] Another consultation that year, on the Holy Spirit, examined similarities and differences among the churches about faith in the Spirit. It found a general willingness to remove the *filioque* ("and the son") from the Nicene Creed, a longstanding issue between eastern and western churches.[21] This discussion was set in the context of Pentecostal and Holiness families of churches, women scholars, and ethical dimensions of ecclesiology. Papers and a statement from the consultation appear in the volume *Spirit of Truth: Ecumenical Perspectives on the Holy Spirit.*[22]

18. David T. Shannon and Gayraud S. Wilmore, eds., *Black Witness to the Apostolic Faith* (Grand Rapids: Eerdmans, 1988).

19. "Toward a Common Expression of Faith: A Black North American Perspective," *Mid-Stream* 24, no. 4 (October 1985): 411-18. *Ecumenical Trends* 14, no. 11 (December 1985): 171-76. Reprinted in Velko and Gros, eds., *Growing Consensus II,* pp. 478-86. For an editorial on the Richmond consultation see Cornish Rogers, "The Gift of Blackness," *The Christian Century,* June 5-12, 1985, pp. 572-73.

20. Paul Fries and Tiran Nersoyan, eds., *Christ in East and West* (Macon, GA: Mercer University Press, 1987). A description of the consultation can be found in *Mid-Stream* 24, no. 4 (October 1985): 457-58. Reprinted using the title "Christological Concerns and the Apostolic Faith," in Velko and Gros, eds., *Growing Consensus II,* pp. 471-77.

21. "Communiqué," *Ecumenical Trends* 15, no. 2 (February 1986): 32-33.

22. Mark Heim and Theodore Stylianopoulos, eds., *Spirit of Truth: Ecumenical Perspectives on the Holy Spirit* (Brookline, MA: Holy Cross Orthodox Press, 1986). The statement only is reprinted under the title "The Holy Spirit Consultation: A Summary Statement," in Burgess and Gros, eds., *Growing Consensus I,* pp. 659-68.

A consultation at Fuller Seminary (1986) co-sponsored by Faith and Order and the David du Plessis Center for Christian Spirituality brought Pentecostal and Holiness perspectives on the Holy Spirit together with those of Catholics, Protestants, and Orthodox. Black church and Latin American perspectives were also represented. The papers appear in *Confessing the Apostolic Faith: Pentecostal Churches and the Ecumenical Movement*.[23] It should be noted that Faith and Order revived the comparative methodology used before Lund for this consultation and two others in 1991 and 1995 in order to help member churches better understand Pentecostals and help Pentecostal scholars find points of contact with member churches.[24] After this, Pentecostals were routinely incorporated in the work of Faith and Order.

The study group on the apostolic faith prepared a study guide on the Nicene Creed for parish and other groups.[25] The group's volume *Apostolic Faith in America* characterizes the American context and ways the apostolic faith is perceived in our diverse Christian traditions.[26]

Encouraged by the commission, now led by Melanie May of the Church of the Brethren, the study group next looked into possibilities of understanding and teaching church history ecumenically. Consultations were arranged to look at the church in the fourth century and in

23. Cecil M. Robeck, ed., *Confessing the Apostolic Faith: Pentecostal Churches and the Ecumenical Movement*. The book is a special issue of *Pneuma: The Journal for the Society of Pentecostal Studies* 9, no. 1 (Spring 1987); also in *One in Christ* 23, nos. 1 and 2 (1987): 61-156. Reprinted in Burgess and Gros, eds., *Ecumenical Documents IV*, pp. 484-90. An account of the consultation appears in Alexandra Brown, "Confessing the Apostolic Faith: The Pentecostal Contribution," *Journal of Ecumenical Studies* 23 (Fall 1986): 779-81. For a history of Faith and Order dialogue with Pentecostals in the U.S. see Jeffrey Gros, F.S.C., "A Pilgrimage in the Spirit: Pentecostal Testimony in the Faith and Order Movement," *Pneuma* 25, no. 1 (Spring 2003).

24. A description of the 1991 consultation appears in Jeffrey Gros, F.S.C., "A Pilgrimage in the Spirit: Pentecostal Testimony in the Faith and Order Movement," *Pneuma: The Journal of the Society for Pentecostal Studies* 25, no. 1 (Spring 2003): 47-49. A description of the 1995 consultation appears in Jeffrey Gros, F.S.C., "Pentecostal Engagement in the Wider Christian Community," *Mid-Stream* 38, no. 4 (1999): 26-74.

25. *Confessing One Faith: Grounds for a Common Witness* (Cincinnati: Forward Movement Publications, 1988).

26. Thaddeus D. Horgan, ed., *Apostolic Faith in America* (Grand Rapids: Eerdmans, 1988).

the nineteenth century, two of the key dividing moments in history. *Faith to Creed* came from the 1989 consultation on the historical and cultural setting of the Nicene Creed, which sought a common understanding of the faith in the fourth century and today.[27] *The Church in the Movement of the Spirit* is from the 1991 consultation on nineteenth-century American-born expressions of the apostolic faith.[28] This drew Campbellite, Pentecostal, African American, Adventist, and an array of Wesleyan, Holiness, and Methodist churches together with confessional Protestant, Orthodox, and Catholic colleagues. *Telling the Churches' Stories: Perspectives on Writing Christian History* presents principles for writing church history ecumenically plus a selection of trial runs showing the principles in operation.[29]

Unity and Renewal of Human Community

Another accomplishment of the Lima Faith and Order meeting (1982) was to place the concern for church unity in the broader horizon of its implications for service and mission in the world. The vehicle for this was a study on The Unity of the Church and the Renewal of Human Community. Consultations were planned in Africa, Asia, the Caribbean, Latin America, Eastern and Western Europe, and North America to bring more voices, experiences, and insights into the search for visible unity. After almost a decade of work, a report titled Church and

27. S. Mark Heim, ed., *Faith to Creed: Ecumenical Perspectives on the Affirmation of the Apostolic Faith in the Fourth Century* (Grand Rapids: Eerdmans, 1991). The statement only is reprinted as "Faith to Creed Consultation: Summary Statement," in Burgess and Gros, eds., *Growing Consensus I*, pp. 669-71.

28. William W. Barr and Rena M. Yocum, eds., *The Church in the Movement of the Spirit* (Grand Rapids: Eerdmans, 1994). A narrative of the consultation by Elizabeth Mellon appears in *Journal of Ecumenical Studies* 28, no. 1 (1991): 369-72. See also Ted A. Campbell, Ann K. Riggs, and Gilbert W. Stafford, eds., *Ancient Faith and American Born Churches* (New York: Paulist Press, 2006).

29. Timothy J. Wengert and Charles W. Brockwell Jr., eds., *Telling the Churches' Stories: Ecumenical Perspectives on Writing Christian History* (Grand Rapids: Eerdmans, 1995). An account of the project is in O. C. Edwards, "The Ecumenical Church Historiography Project," *Ecumenical Trends* 21, no. 2 (February 1992): 28-32.

World would be submitted to the churches in 1990 for study and response.

The North American consultation was held in Harlem in 1988, jointly sponsored by World Council and National Council Faith and Order. The task was to bring the African American church perspective to bear on the international study and to bring international Orthodox, Protestant, and Catholic theologians into direct dialogue with and experience of African American worship, church life, and theology. Participants from African American, Baptist, Methodist, and Pentecostal churches were joined by African Americans from predominantly white Catholic and Protestant churches. The consultation produced recommendations to the churches and to Faith and Order in the world and national councils.[30]

A U.S. Faith and Order working group on Unity and Renewal, chaired by Letty M. Russell and Robert J. Schreiter, C.P.P.S., followed a contextual methodology as distinct from the more usual convergence methodology. This meant beginning with the experience of projects or organizations engaged in some aspect of the struggle for human renewal whose work was informed by Christian commitment and ecumenical cooperation. *Changing Contexts of Faith* was published in order to help congregations, ecumenical groups, and social action task forces do theology, in the belief that questions of faith come alive when joined with action and experience in specific contexts.[31] The group focused on the AIDS epidemic and the ministry of the church with people having AIDS, which resulted in the volume *The Church with AIDS: Renewal in the Midst of Crisis.*[32]

By placing previously marginalized persons or issues at the center

30. "Listening and Learning in Harlem: The WCC Faith and Order/Black Churches in the U.S. Consultation," *Mid-Stream* 28, no. 4 (October 1989): 333-68, 412-20. Reprinted under the title "Report of the Harlem (1988) Consultation on Unity and Renewal with Black Churches in the USA," in Burgess and Gros, eds., *Growing Consensus I,* pp. 649-58.

31. Letty M. Russell, ed., *Changing Contexts of Faith* (Philadelphia: Fortress Press, 1985). See also Letty M. Russell, "Unity and Renewal in Feminist Perspective," *Mid-Stream* 27, no. 1 (January 1988): 55-66.

32. Letty M. Russell, ed., *The Church with AIDS: Renewal in the Midst of Crisis* (Louisville: Westminster/John Knox Press, 1990).

of its work, this group sought to understand how shifting the center alters the nature and content of theological reflection on the unity of the church. The volume *Women and Church: The Challenge of Ecumenical Solidarity in an Age of Alienation* celebrates the World Council's Ecumenical Decade of Churches in Solidarity with Women (1988-1998); raises questions about current practices, structures of ministry, and new models; and discusses authority and its abuse in the church and the corrective of mutual empowerment.[33] Starting in 1989 the group studied white racism or supremacy as a church-uniting or church-dividing issue. Their volume *Ending Racism in the Church* deals with the sin of racism as it affects relationships between African American and European American Christians and as it undermines the gospel.[34]

This was a time when black churches were being burned deliberately. The National Council's response included the publication *Out of the Ashes: Burned Churches and the Community of Faith,* edited by Norman A. Hjelm.[35]

Canberra: Unity as *Koinonia*

The seventh assembly of the World Council, meeting at Canberra in 1991, brought forward another statement of the goal of visible unity titled The Unity of the Church as Koinonia: Gift and Calling. It presents the triune communion of the life and purpose of God of which the church is a foretaste, sign, and servant. Yet the churches are not only divided but "satisfied to co-exist in division," which contradicts their "very nature" and costs them the credibility of their witness. A characterization is offered of the future and already given unity of the church as *koinonia:*

---

33. Melanie A. May, ed., *Women and Church: The Challenge of Ecumenical Solidarity in an Age of Alienation* (Grand Rapids: Eerdmans and New York: Friendship Press, 1991).

34. Susan E. Davies and Sister Paul Teresa Hennessee, S.A., eds., *Ending Racism in the Church* (Cleveland: United Church Press, 1998).

35. Norman A. Hjelm, ed., *Out of the Ashes: Burned Churches and the Community of Faith* (Nashville: Thomas Nelson, 1997).

The unity of the church to which we are called is a koinonia given and expressed in the common confession of the apostolic faith; a common sacramental life entered by the one baptism and celebrated together in one eucharistic fellowship; a common life in which members and ministries are mutually recognized and reconciled; and a common mission witnessing to the gospel of God's grace to all people and serving the whole of creation. The goal of the search for full communion is realized when all the churches are able to recognize in one another the one, holy, catholic and apostolic Church in its fulness. This full communion will be expressed on the local and the universal levels through conciliar forms of life and action. In such communion churches are bound in all aspects of their life together at all levels in confessing the one faith and engaging in worship and witness, deliberation and action.

Diversities that are rooted in theological traditions, various cultural, ethnic or historical contexts are integral to the nature of communion; yet there are limits to diversity. Diversity is illegitimate when, for instance, it makes impossible the common confession of Jesus Christ as God and Savior the same yesterday, today and forever (Heb. 13:8); salvation and the final destiny of humanity as proclaimed in Holy Scripture and preached by the apostolic community. In communion diversities are brought together in harmony as gifts of the Holy Spirit, contributing to the richness and fulness of the church of God.[36]

The statement voices the assembly's desire for better ecumenical practice, calling the churches to do these things:

1. recognize each other's baptisms on the basis of BEM;
2. move toward recognition of the apostolic faith as expressed through the Nicene-Constantinopolitan Creed;
3. on the basis of such convergences explicitly to consider forms of eucharistic hospitality;

36. Michael Kinnamon, ed., *Signs of the Spirit: Official Report of the Seventh Assembly* (Geneva: WCC and Grand Rapids: Eerdmans, 1991), pp. 172-74.

4. move towards a mutual recognition of ministries;
5. undertake common witness;
6. link the search for sacramental communion with the work for justice, peace, and the integrity of creation;
7. help parishes express in appropriate ways locally the degree of communion that already exists.

Tensions arose at this assembly around elections of council presidents and committees to function until the next assembly. This may suggest another obstacle to *koinonia:* when some in the community perceive that they are insufficiently represented in church councils or leadership.

Ecclesiology

Norman A. Hjelm of the Evangelical Lutheran Church in America succeeded Gros as director in 1991, but in a part-time capacity because of council finances.

A study group on Ecclesiology set to work on the interconnected topics of ecclesiology, *koinonia,* and ministry in 1991. Soon another topic appeared more pressing. The governing board appointed an ecclesiology task force as part of an effort to reflect on the ecclesial character of the council of churches, to examine the motivation in the ecclesiologies of the member churches for ecumenical life and work, and to consider what a more adequate future ecumenical expression might be. The hope was to clarify the nature and basis of ecumenical relationships among a wider circle of American churches. Since Faith and Order included representatives of a number of churches not now members of the council, it might be in a position to see what changes would make their membership possible. So the Faith and Order study group held two consultations in 1994 on the perspectives of nonmember bodies and the possibility of a "table" for intentional relationships, but the findings on the latter were not encouraging.[37] The final statement of the

37. *Ecumenical Trends* 25, no. 2 (February 1996): 25-28.

governing board task force, led by Michael Kinnamon with staff support from Faith and Order, was in three sections: Reclaiming the Vision, Deepening Our Commitment, and Expanding the Table.[38]

In principle the National Council was an ecumenical expression for all Christians; in practice it included only a fraction of them. It may not be amiss to see the council in this situation as an unwilling sign of nineteenth-century American and earlier divisions. The task force proposed a "table" made up of leaders from all Christian bodies in the nation. In fact, a very private gathering of such leaders had been meeting periodically for many years, but on the strict understanding that it reach no agreements and its discussions be off the record. No public table materialized in this decade as an expression of and witness to Christian unity as a result of these efforts (see below). A judgment in the 1964 Faith and Order study of The Ecclesiological Significance of Councils of Churches was still relevant:

> The council of churches movement is itself in need of self-criticism and purification, which must take the form of increasingly direct confrontation of the question of the reunion of the Church (as distinguished from the cooperation of churches). As they press the ecclesiological question, the councils of churches cannot expect to remain unchanged themselves.[39]

The Faith and Order group on Ecclesiology subsequently worked on a commentary on the church as *koinonia,* based on the report of the world conference at Santiago de Compostela, but issued no publication.

Santiago de Compostela: Fuller *Koinonia*

The fifth world conference on Faith and Order — the first in the thirty years since Montreal — gathered in the pilgrimage city of Santiago de Compostela, Spain, in 1993. The increase in number of churches partic-

---

38. *Ecumenical Trends* 27, no. 7 (July-August 1998): 97-108.
39. Burgess and Gros, eds., *Growing Consensus I,* pp. 581-613, quote on p. 610.

ipating, the number of woman and younger theologians, and people from all regions of the world was dramatic.

Santiago set out to explore the significance for the churches' *koinonia* of the three long-range studies completed since Montreal: Baptism, Eucharist and Ministry (1982), Church and World (1990), and Confessing the Apostolic Faith Today (1991). Another purpose was to offer steps the churches needed to take in order to receive these convergences into their life. In preparation a team gathered insights from Canberra, a series of nine continental consultations, and other sources in a paper on the theme Towards Koinonia in Faith, Life and Witness.

Statements from assemblies prior to Canberra about the goal of visible unity were thought to be too easily misunderstood as seeking to enforce uniformity and a monocultural approach. They needed to be transformed through (1) an understanding of the church as God's instrument for restoring community in all creation and (2) by an emphasis on church unity as relational and many-dimensioned. Such a process of transformation was seen as ongoing and complex. The conference message commended this work of transformation to the churches for study and action, and to the Faith and Order commission for its future planning.[40]

Ecumenical Reception

Following up on earlier work on multilateral and bilateral dialogues, a study group on Ecumenical Reception prepared the report *Twelve Tales Untold: A Study Guide for Ecumenical Reception*.[41] Twelve case studies show how ecumenical agreements can be incorporated in the faith and life of the people of God. Although the group also discussed how to help congregations understand the message from Santiago de Compostela, no publication ensued.

The study group proposed that a ministry task force be created, as

40. Thomas F. Best and Gunther Gassmann, eds., *On the Way to Fuller Koinonia* (Geneva: WCC, 1994), pp. 225-27.

41. John T. Ford and Darlis J. Swan, *Twelve Tales Untold: A Study Guide for Ecumenical Reception* (Grand Rapids: Eerdmans, 1993).

had the earlier study group on reception of BEM. The resulting task force co-sponsored a consultation in 1988 on the Diaconate with the Roman Catholic diocese of Fort Worth, Texas. The intention was to assist the churches in the reception of BEM, the COCU Consensus, and bilateral dialogues on the ministry. Part of this work was taken over by an independent national diaconate group.

Peace Witness

The Apostolic Faith study already mentioned took up the claim of the historic peace churches that the church's witness to peace is an essential element in confessing the apostolic faith. Consultations at Bethany Theological Seminary (1990) and in Douglaston, New York (1991), considered the scriptural basis for peace witness, the use of scripture in statements on peace by major U.S. church assemblies, nonviolence in early Christianity, the rise of churches with a commitment to pacifism or nonviolence as a mark of the church (especially Mennonites, Quakers, Brethren), and twentieth-century dialogue between the historic peace traditions and other churches. This work is detailed in *The Church's Peace Witness* and the earlier volume *Faith to Creed*.[42]

A further consultation was sponsored jointly by Faith and Order and the Joan B. Kroc Institute for International Peace, University of Notre Dame, in 1995. The consultation's fuller explorations, points of contention, and recommendations are captured in the volume *The Fragmentation of the Church and Its Unity in Peace-making*.[43]

42. The report and supporting essays are in Marlin E. Miller and Barbara Nelson Gingerich, eds., *The Church's Peace Witness* (Grand Rapids: Eerdmans, 1994). The report only is reprinted under the title "The Apostolic Faith and the Church's Peace Witness: A Summary Statement," in Velko and Gros, eds., *Growing Consensus II*, pp. 496-503. S. Mark Heim, ed., *Faith to Creed* (Grand Rapids: Eerdmans, 1991). The 1990 consultation is described in Jeffrey Gros, "Expressing the Apostolic Faith: The Peace Churches' Contribution," *Ecumenical Trends* 19, no. 6 (June 1990): 92-94.

43. The report and background essays are in Jeffrey Gros and John D. Rempel, eds., *The Fragmentation of the Church and Its Unity in Peace-making* (Grand Rapids: Eerdmans, 2001). The report is reprinted in *One in Christ* 31, no. 4 (1995): 379-85; *The*

Religious Pluralism

A Faith and Order study group devoted eight years to an exploration of the churches' responses to religious pluralism. A consultation was arranged in 1995 with the National Council commission on Interfaith Relations to hear from a dozen Christian traditions and gather theological resources for interreligious dialogue and for living with pluralism. Papers and discussion are printed in *Grounds for Understanding: Ecumenical Resources for Responses to Religious Pluralism.*[44]

Two other consultations were arranged in cooperation with the Institute of Ecumenical and Cultural Research at St. John's University, Collegeville, Minnesota. The publications are *Confessing Christian Faith in a Pluralistic Society* and *Living Faith Fully in the United States Today.*[45]

The study group also reviewed ecumenical theologies of Christian mission produced over the last century with regard to religious pluralism and interfaith relations but produced no publication.

Justification and the Future of the Ecumenical Movement

William G. Rusch of the Evangelical Lutheran Church in America became sixth director, and Paul Meyendorff of the Orthodox Church in America was elected chairman of the commission in 1996. In 2000 Meyendorff and Susan E. Davies of the United Church of Christ became co-chairs of the commission.

Faith and Order sponsored a conference on Justification and the Future of the Ecumenical Movement with Yale University in 2000. Based on the 1999 Joint Declaration on the Doctrine of Justification

---

Ecumenical Review 48, no. 1 (January 1996): 122-24; and Velko and Gros, eds., *Growing Consensus II,* pp. 504-10.

44. S. Mark Heim, ed., *Grounds for Understanding: Ecumenical Resources for Responses to Religious Pluralism* (New York: Paulist Press, 1998).

45. *Confessing Christian Faith in a Pluralistic Society* (Collegeville, MN: Institute for Ecumenical and Cultural Research, 1995). *Living Faith Fully in the United States Today* (Collegeville, MN: Institute for Ecumenical and Cultural Research, 2001).

from the Lutheran–Roman Catholic International Study Commission, this was the first exploration of the potential significance of this historic declaration for the churches. A report and papers are in the volume *Justification and the Future of the Ecumenical Movement: The Joint Declaration on the Doctrine of Justification.*[46]

Full Communion Agreements

Churches of different traditions or confessions were moving toward full communion relationships at this time. In 1989 the United Church of Christ and the Christian Church (Disciples of Christ) entered full communion on the basis of agreements in the document Ecumenical Partnership. A merger of their global ministries functions and boards was effected in 1995.

In 1995 the General Conference Mennonite Church and the Mennonite Church entered full communion on the basis of agreements in the document Confession of Faith in a Mennonite Perspective. They merged to form the Mennonite Church USA in 1999.

In 1997 three Reformed churches (Presbyterian Church [USA], Reformed Church in America, United Church of Christ) and the Evangelical Lutheran Church in America entered full communion on the basis of agreements in the document A Common Calling. The agreement in faith, sacraments, and mission was prepared by the Lutheran-Reformed dialogue in the United States using work of dialogues between the Lutheran World Federation and the World Alliance of Reformed Churches as well as dialogues underlying the Leuenberg Agreement between European Lutheran and Reformed churches.

In 1999 the Episcopal Church and the Evangelical Lutheran Church in America entered into full communion on the basis of agreements in the document Called to Common Mission on the ordained ministry as well as on faith, sacraments, and mission. Called to Com-

---

46. William G. Rusch, ed., *Justification and the Future of the Ecumenical Movement: The Joint Declaration on the Doctrine of Justification* (Collegeville, MN: Liturgical Press, 2003).

mon Mission was a revision of the Concordat of Agreement prepared by the Lutheran-Episcopal dialogue in the United States. This used work of the Anglican-Lutheran International Conversations as well as dialogues that led to the Porvoo Common Statement adopted by Anglican churches of England, Ireland, and Wales, and five Nordic and Baltic Lutheran churches.

In 1999 the Evangelical Lutheran Church in America and the Moravian Church entered full communion on the basis of agreements in the document Following Our Shepherd to Full Communion.

This remarkable development of full communion agreements led Faith and Order in 2000 to begin a study of concepts of unity and full communion as understood in different churches as well as in proposals from the Consultation on Church Union. A progress report to the commission in 2000 on problems with the meaning of full communion was authored by O. C. Edwards Jr. and later appeared as a preface to a collection of the agreements. The final report of the study will appear on the Faith and Order page of the National Council website in two issues edited by Lorelei Fuchs, S.A., and Douglas Foster.[47]

In 1999 the Consultation on Church Union met after seven member churches had approved the two documents The COCU Consensus and Churches in Covenant Communion, but the Episcopal and Presbyterian churches had not. In this situation the representatives of the participating churches undertook a description of the current relationships between these churches. They decided to change the longstanding title of the consultation to Churches Uniting in Christ at a public declaration and liturgical celebration. A new document, "Marks" of Churches Uniting in Christ, listed nine visible marks and envisioned a process leading toward "fuller unity," including work toward a time when the ministries of each participating church might become one ministry. A document titled Call to Christian Commitment and Action to Combat Racism established a priority in this area. A desire for dialogue in ever-widening circles was expressed, including Catholic, Or-

47. Velko and Gros, eds., *Growing Consensus II*, pp. 5-124. See also O. C. Edwards Jr., "Meanings of Full Communion: The Essence of Life in the Body," *Speaking of Unity* 1, nos. 1/2/3 (2005), ncccusa.org.

thodox, Lutheran, Pentecostal, Holiness, and Baptist traditions and with other, historic black churches. Later a new category, "partners in mission and dialogue," was created to encourage churches wishing to maintain a relationship to CUIC other than full membership.

Another North American Conference

A consultation in 1999 considered the feasibility of a second North American Conference on Faith and Order. Next year the commission approved "movement" based on a conference to promote the visible unity and mission of the churches. Rusch resigned in 2001 to develop a plan and was succeeded as seventh director by Ann K. Riggs of the Friends General Conference. In view of the limited Faith and Order budget and after an unsuccessful National Council effort to secure a planning grant, a nonprofit foundation was created. Its committee issued A Call to the Churches for a conference in 2005.

The projected goals and purposes of the conference and the preliminary local and national study process were (1) "to reach new insights regarding the faith, order, and worship of the church, doing so on the one hand to enhance the *unity* of the churches and on the other to further the *identity* of each church" in order to "help re-energize the churches and their people at this time"; (2) "to enable the churches to be better equipped to carry out their mission in light of the relevant social, religious, cultural, and racial factors that confront them in the contemporary North American and global contexts"; and (3) to promote the search for unity throughout the churches by such means as enlisting new partners, preparing a new generation of ecumenical leaders, reflecting on the structures of conciliar ecumenism, assisting in the ongoing reception of ecumenical results, etc.

The foundation, working with limited resources, consulted with church leadership. Some strongly encouraged the project, but the foundation concluded in 2006 that interest and financial support for a major conference were insufficient to continue efforts. We note, however, that this brief history of Faith and Order in the United States originated as preparation for the conference.

Authority of the Church in the World

Beginning in 2000 the commission launched a study on Authority in the Church. When Pope John Paul II's statement *Ut Unum Sint* appeared, asking for contributions on how the pope might better serve the unity of the churches, the commission prepared a response for the Pontifical Council for the Promotion of Christian Unity.[48]

The study turned to consider The Authority of the Church in the World, bringing together voices from a wide spectrum of Christian bodies on the nature of the church's authority and its application in witness as these affect church divisions and movements toward visible unity. While serious differences were noted, the study found much on which the churches agree. A few papers were published along the way, and a consensus document and twenty-four denominational papers appears on the Faith and Order page of the National Council website, edited by Antonios Kireopoulos.[49]

The publication *Love for the Poor: God's Love for the Poor and the Church's Witness to It*[50] was stimulated by work on the hermeneutics of word and practice at the World Council assembly held at Harare (1998). Chapters examine the scriptural witness, insights from early centuries, the spirituality of justice, heroes of the faith, and an ethic of justice-making. Since "no single church can do these things alone," by acting together "the church can model its unity in the world in ministries to the poor."

In 2004 Davies and O. C. Edwards of the Episcopal Church were elected co-chairs of the commission. Antonios Kireopoulos of the Greek Orthodox Church succeeded Riggs as eighth director in 2008.

---

48. Velko and Gros, eds., *Growing Consensus II*, pp. 511-18, www.ncccusa.org.

49. "Authority of the Church in the World: Preview," *Ecumenical Trends* 31, no. 8 (September 2002): 113-26, www.ncccusa.org.

50. Shaun Casey, John Crossin, O.S.F.S., Eric H. Crump, A. Katherine Grieb, Beverly Mitchell, and Ann K. Riggs, *Love for the Poor: God's Love for the Poor and the Church's Witness to It* (New York: National Council of the Churches of Christ, Friendship Press, 2005).

CHAPTER III

Looking Back/Ahead

In 2007 a large gathering at Oberlin, Ohio, celebrated the fiftieth anniversary of the North American Conference on Faith and Order. Its theme was On Being Christians Together, implying that the honor owed the ecumenical movement's ample heritage would not overshadow the work needed to open doors to unity now. The book of essays titled *Some Ecumenical Directions in the U.S. Today: Churches on a Theological Journey* is a product.[1]

The North American Conference at Oberlin in 1957 occurred in a now oddly distant North America. The population is now much larger and far more diverse. American culture has changed and we are in the digital age. The position and influence of the "mainline" churches have lessened. Today the Faith and Order commission reflects these and other changes. As many as eighty traditions were present for the fiftieth anniversary celebration.

One of the aims of Faith and Order is to dispose of misunderstandings and arrive at a more complete and precise knowledge of the foundations of faith on all sides. Otherwise each small, middle-size, or large communion may understand only itself, not realizing that the commitments of others may not need to come at the expense of their own. Much headway has been made in the last fifty years. The climate of relation-

---

1. *Some Ecumenical Directions in the U.S. Today: Churches on a Theological Journey,* ed. Anthony Kireopoulos and Julia M. Mecera (Mahwah, NJ: Paulist Press, 2011).

ships between communions has improved markedly. Another aim is agreement in faith, order, and worship. The many agreed statements produced by international and national dialogues between the main traditions and the voluminous theological and historical studies produced by scholars demonstrate that historic obstacles to reconciliation of the communions are giving way, even as new issues arise in new circumstances.

These developments have enabled communions to take significant steps toward visible unity since Oberlin: (1) although the South India model of church union did not succeed, three unions occurred between communions of the same tradition or confession; (2) communions initiated full communion relationships between Episcopal and Lutheran, Lutheran and Reformed, Lutheran and Moravian, and United Church of Christ and Christian Church (Disciples of Christ) traditions or confessions; (3) agreements were reached or proposed for nine communions in Churches Uniting in Christ; and (4) nine American Orthodox churches belonging to eastern European and middle-eastern patriarchates formed a Standing Conference of Canonical Orthodox Bishops.

Meanwhile the Christian World Communions witnessed to catholicity not least through the reports of international dialogues. Especially notable are the Lutheran–Roman Catholic Joint Declaration on the Doctrine of Justification by Faith addressing the focal issue of the sixteenth-century Reformation, and the joint theological reports of the Orthodox and the Oriental Orthodox churches addressing doctrinal issues of this earliest division.

Dialogues and other work in world, regional, national, and local councils are now more complex. Beginning with Oberlin in 1957, Faith and Order took into account cultural factors, scholarly disciplines beyond theology, and contributions of younger people. In response to the Second Vatican Council, Faith and Order welcomed the Roman Catholic tradition and sought relations with Evangelical communions. Contextual and case study methods illuminated racial, ethnic, and gender issues and also local experiments. The Civil Rights movement brought issues of African American theologians to prominence. The women's movement brought the leadership of women theologians with new perspectives on various issues. A surging Hispanic population promises further perspectives. Such developments have led to better understanding of differences (and opportunities), while achieving consensus has become more demanding. Consultations with scholars from "American-born" Pentecostal, Holiness, and Adventist communions and from African American and peace communions have supplied missing information. Empowerment of new players and new perspectives has changed the ecumenical movement in the United States in ways that will unfold for generations to come.

Slower to change are the relationships between ecumenically engaged communions and many Evangelical and Pentecostal churches and communities. Faith and Order has pioneered, but ecumenically concerned communions and councils need to intensify engagement with "American-born" communions. Charismatic members in ecumenically engaged communions aid dialogue with Pentecostals.

The presence of communions together in local, state, and national councils or conferences is important as a sign of the *degree* of existing *koinonia*/communion. People need something to see and hear and touch, and that something must be embodied in human/institutional form — however provisional — to make possible the special sympathy and mutuality that are the basis of human community. Efforts to transform the National Council to accord with the wider horizon of contemporary ecumenism have been unsuccessful so far. Negotiations for a new body will be needed when the time comes. Precedent for this is the mid-twentieth-century supplanting of the earlier Federal Council by the National Council. In our multicultural nation it is hard to know what form a new body should take. A forum was proposed recently to be called Churches Together in the U.S.A., aimed at helping churches and Christian organizations to "grow together in Christ" and be strengthened. Experience of participation in some such wider body may show the way.

Purpose of the Church

Over the last half-century and more, World Council Faith and Order, and World Christian Communions in a different way, have worked to clarify the goal of visible unity. It is becoming clear that unity and diversity are not opposites; rather, unity is discerned through legitimate diversity. New generations will bring further diversities because of new circumstances, testing them against the essential unity of the church. More agreements about faith, sacraments, ministry, mission, and decision-making are needed, together with processes for their reception in communions. Above all, new venues for the people of God to experience *koinonia*/communion are needed.

National Council Faith and Order cannot hope to describe any *terminus* for visible unity among the plurality of communions in our nation of immigrants. Yet there is a growing realization that visible or tangible unity is part of the identity or purpose of the church. Faith and Order points to qualities, recognizable features, or characteristic marks of a future place where historic communions — some ancient, some born in America — may be seen to share the purpose of the church. Fairly concrete hopes are needed if there is to be movement. Options must be interesting enough to capture and sustain attention. Response in the communions may be halting and slow. In other words, future ecumenical developments will not be unlike those of the past fifty years: various and cumulative.

Historical studies demonstrate that there was never a time of perfect church unity. Seeking its unity in every age is part of the purpose of the church. Serving the whole purpose of the church must be the aim of all Christians. It includes love, faith, hope, unity, worship, doctrine, peace, evangelism, justice, and more. This means Faith and Order must seek every means of partnership with leadership of communions in congregations, synods/dioceses, and the nation. Communities cohere through coming together for certain ends. Unity comes as Christians serve the church's God-given purpose, and in that we see the Holy Spirit's work even now.

Still More Voices

A large question remains. The distribution of power in the world is slowly passing away from U.S. dominance. Commentators say the West is waning and the rest are rising. Power in the world is becoming more decentralized and interconnected, and is defined and directed from many places and by many people. Does this point to an enhanced function for global communions, which have already demonstrated a capacity for dialogue? How will U.S. communions adjust to these changes? Will cultural isolation and ecclesiastical independence both wane and closer ties rise with communions in other cultures? Will we strengthen consultation, cooperation, and correlation with others or will we talk to ourselves? Together with the others, will we cultivate and energize respectful global interreligious relationships?

Findings of the National Faith and Order Colloquium on "Salvation and Life"

NOTE: "Men" was used at this time in an inclusive sense to mean women and men.

Shared Convictions

Men in our day cry for help. Some men cry aloud; some in their groping or despair are inarticulate. Sometimes men are most concerned over their immediate and tangible needs or dangers, sometimes over their pervasive and ultimate needs or dangers. Some men, when they cry to be delivered, would say they wish to be "saved" from their dangers or needs; others dislike to use that term. Millions of men seek, and some apparently find their satisfaction, happiness or fulfillment quite outside the Christian community or Christian faith.

For ages upon ages, in various ways, men have cried for help. Jesus Christ came exactly to serve the poor and disinherited, the imprisoned, the blind, the broken-hearted, the oppressed. Christ's disciples today bear responsibility to serve all men in their needs, their misery, their lostness. Christians are responsible to discern the specific forms which poverty, imprisonment, blindness, broken-heartedness and oppression take in today's world, and to serve these suffering people in the name of Jesus Christ. Moreover, men are not only victims of circumstances. They are also people who have strayed from God and rebelled against

Him, men who need His forgiveness and reconciliation. The mandate of this Faith and Order Colloquium, therefore, comes both from the cries of men in urgent need and from the urgent call of our Lord Jesus Christ to follow Him.

Christians see their task in terms of the good news of salvation for men, because they follow a Lord who came "to seek and to save." Our Colloquium has concentrated on the theme "Salvation and Life" in order to reexamine what Christian discipleship means in the present-day tasks of Christians and of the Christian church. We must therefore say something, in a preliminary way, of what we understand by salvation, before we can state our present findings on the problems of sharing the good news of salvation with the world today.

1. God, who made the world, loves all men and cares about all men. His will is true life for all men.

2. In Jesus of Nazareth God, who is always in action to express His love and care for men, came personally into human life and shared our human struggle. In fulfillment of God's love for men Jesus died and rose again, and through the Holy Spirit He now lives among us, continuing to help us share in His mission.

3. Not only is salvation revealed decisively in Jesus Christ; it is a decisive change accomplished by Christ. Since He died and rose for all men, there is a sense in which He achieved a change in the relation of all men to God; the whole world is reconciled to God and redeemed from evil. Men who truly place their trust in Christ and give their lively allegiance to Him experience a radical change in their lives. They obtain a truly new life; in some real sense they share in the life of the resurrected Christ. In Christ they are no longer lost but found; they know to whom they belong: this is the glorious liberty of the sons of God.

4. This divine gift of salvation or new life, which men could not earn by themselves but which has been given them by God's inexpressible love, is a gift not to privilege but to a life-long task: a sharing in Christ's task of serving the world. It is not a possession over which we dispose; it is a trust for which we are held accountable. This present salvation gives a new breadth and new urgency to our life-

87

task, but also a new power and support to meet the responsibility to love men as Christ loves them. It gives us release from selfishness, joy in living and serving and sharing our new life, hope in our struggles, and patience and forbearance in our sufferings. It is never a finished thing in this life; not only do we make mistakes, we constantly need forgiveness and restoration for our sinful failures to live according to our faith; but we have Christ with us to guide and chasten us and enable us to grow. Salvation looks forward to a consummation beyond all our striving and our imagining.

5. Salvation or new life in Christ is never a private or solitary experience. We receive new life by being adopted into the family of God, or incorporated into "the body of Christ." Man is not truly man, except as he is man-in-community. The church is the new community in Christ. This fellowship of believers cannot be perfectly identified with the institutional church in the world, but neither can it be separated from it as if the true church were merely some invisible ideal. It was to a real community of believers that Christ entrusted His mission to the world and gave His promise to be with the faithful community. Like the individual believer, the church bears the good news of Christ's saving and serving love to the world, inviting men to be reconciled to God through Jesus Christ. Like the individual believer, the church is formed by the living God and His promise, but it also needs to grow by God's grace. Moreover, the fellowship whose task it is to call all human society to account is itself called to account by God; judgment begins with the household of God. God's judgment continually calls the churches to repentant action. Not only in the matter of understanding itself and its task, but also and more urgently in the matter of decision and action, wisdom and courage, the church constantly needs to grow.

6. Through Christ we learn in a new way that Christians are members of one worldwide human family, in which they have a distinctive mission. Though they are not to be "conformed to the world," they are to show forth in the world what God's intention is for the whole human community. The Christian is truly a man-in-community not by simply belonging to the church, but rather by

living out his faith with his fellow-Christians as new men in the world. The church should seek urgently to understand her mission under the Cross as that of a saving and healing community. She should respond to every human crisis by acting with compassion, wisdom and courage.

7. Christians should be open to God's truth wherever it is found, and open to all men as brothers, respecting and loving them even where they disagree with their beliefs and the values they cherish. We are now realizing that we have understood God's loving will too narrowly. Through Jesus Christ we are learning not only that we have often acted lovelessly but that we have tended to view God's love more restrictively than Jesus did. We are therefore trying to discern the true nature and scope of God's will toward all men, and the ways to put this love into practice. This is the task of our Colloquium.

The State of the Question

Among the varied tasks and modes of ecumenical theologizing, one which has been the specific burden of Faith and Order has been the testing of the continuity which present statements of faith, in their diversity and even contradiction, claim with historic Christianity.

The ethos of Faith and Order addresses, respectfully but rigorously, the differences between Christian traditions, seeking to develop a hermeneutic for dealing with their sometimes contradictory truth claims. In North America, where we have the phenomenon of theological traditions crossing denominational lines, the plurality of competing traditions cannot be dealt with as if "traditions" strictly coincide with "denominations."

In our discussion of Salvation and Life we support the search for formulations sufficiently multifaceted to reflect *legitimate diversity* of conviction and emphasis. In seeking such formulations we become aware that there are limits to diversity of conviction and emphasis beyond which legitimacy can no longer be established; that is to say, there is a point at which diversity can become disruptive discontinuity.

A. Misleading Antitheses

    1. It is misleading to set individual salvation against the salvation of society, as though we had to choose one against the other. These dimensions of salvation are related: the real question is *how*.

    2. It is also misleading to set the study of contemporary man in opposition to the study of the biblical diagnosis of man, as though the question of the relevance of the Christian doctrine of man could be settled at either point without the other. Though theologians may specialize in one area or the other, each needs to be cognizant of the other, although the nature of the relationship is still a problem.

B. Distinctions That Clarify

    1. We need to distinguish between two different levels of human hunger — hunger for food, clothing, identity, justice, etc., on the one hand, and hunger for what Matthew 5:6 calls "righteousness" on the other. God is concerned for both. The church as His people is also to be concerned for both. Yet they are not equivalent, for the latter hunger is the ultimate, as Jesus says, in Matthew 4:4 (quoting Deut. 8:3), "Man does not live by bread alone, but by every word that proceeds out of the mouth of God."

    2. We need to distinguish also between the offense given by the empirical church, and the offense of the Gospel. It seems clear enough that the church as institution, clothed in theological clichés that seem meaningless, failing to fulfill its most obvious calling to love, conveying the impression of withdrawal, defensiveness, and even arrogant superiority, has alienated many and incurred the dissatisfaction of its own members and the contempt of the very world it ought to reach. Yet it is not profitable simply to castigate the church, and it is dangerous to imagine that we can deliver ourselves from it by rejecting all that seems offensive or resolving not to be guilty of its faults. For Christ continues to love that church as a holy church, without spot or wrinkle.

    Rather, we need to discover more clearly why many are indifferent to the Gospel itself and why to others it is offensive, for example why anyone would be moved to call Jesus *cursed* rather than Lord (1 Cor. 12:3). For then, perhaps we would know better how to trust, serve, and proclaim Him, for the healing of the church and for the real hope of the world.

C. Questions Remaining

1. Within the process of the Colloquium, the diverse emphases being placed on Christian salvation raise the question whether this danger of discontinuity cannot arise from at least two different directions. Some fear that the quest for relevance in a pluralistic world cannot lead to new formulations and perspectives which break the continuity of the Christian message of salvation. Others fear that fidelity to the past leads to archaism which equally falsifies and breaks with the good news of salvation which Christianity proclaims. It is not yet clear that those who emphatically strive to avoid the first danger and those more emphatic in avoiding the second can at the same time stave off serious disagreement with one another. Here the question of the legitimacy of divergent emphases is keenly experienced and not yet clearly resolved.

2. We affirm that the Christian understanding of salvation entails a present and living hope. Our discussion has disclosed that we have not reached clarity on the nature of that hope as a Christian disposition nor have we been able to express agreement as to the specific content of that hope in terms of its fulfillment. We are not agreed about:

   a. The relation of ultimate hope ("I look for the resurrection of the dead") to hope for tomorrow's new possibilities.

   b. Whether the content of hope can be specified, or whether a mature hope is only the hopeful disposition.

   c. The nature of the relation of personal and social hopes.

3. We affirm that the Christian understanding of salvation entails faith in Jesus Christ as the Agent of God's redemptive activity. Our discussion has disclosed that we are not yet able to express agreement regarding the nature of Christ's role as Savior. Some regard his salvific role in terms of a remem-

bered model from the past (e.g. remembered as "man for others"). Others see His role as present power which determines the nature of the experience of salvation. Some would claim that the quest for salvation cannot begin unless Christ as Savior is encountered. Others would say that Jesus Christ is the answer to the quest for salvation. It is not yet clear that diverse viewpoints such as these eventually can be found in agreement, nor to what depth of disagreement they might lead.

4. We are agreed that the Christian understanding of salvation entails a recognition of the reality of the judgment of God, from which His grace alone can save man. Our discussion has further disclosed that we find unacceptable both a simplistic universalism and an arrogant particularism. Some of us, however, are convinced that Christians must affirm a possibility of salvation for men outside the Christian community; others doubt that such an affirmation is possible.

5. We are agreed that it is necessary to be open to God's truth wherever it may be found among men. We are also committed to communicate the Gospel. But we are not agreed as to how openness to inter-faith dialogue and the commitment to evangelism are to be understood or how they may be reconciled.

6. We are agreed that the Christian understanding of salvation entails a particular assumption about the human condition which requires the intervention of God's saving action. Our discussion has disclosed that some see God's culminating and condemning action as opposite dimensions of one salvific process. Others would see condemnation as the opposite of salvation. This difference of understanding gives to terms in use by the Colloquium, such as "man's lostness" and "God's judgment," a variation in meaning which may thus far be masking still further disagreements or at least still further serious questions as to the meaning of salvation.

7. We note concerning point II, 5 and 6, that the distress of society, the conflict and strife in our time, not least in America, requires a clearer understanding of the relation of the Gospel to

nations than is here expressed. Can cultures as cultures, nations as nations, be saved from decay, sin and destruction? Some of us believe that by God's grace they can, others disagree, but to see whether this is possible and what salvation entails for the church requires clearer thinking about the relation of God to evolution, to violence, to oppression, to social processes of crisis in general.

Index

94

Index